PRAISE FOR *BIBLICAL GRANDPARENTING*

I give my highest endorsement to this much-needed book. Rarely do we find thinking that is this prophetic, original, scholarly and biblical in one place. **Josh Mulvihill has cut through our culture's views on grandparenting to give Christian grandparents a clear vision of their unique role in the next generation's lives.** I hope it will be widely read, discussed and responded to in ways that change the very fabric of this country and the grandparenting culture.

VALERIE BELL
CEO, Awana and Author of Faith-Shaped Kids

Biblical Grandparenting provides a look at what God's Word says about the role of grandparents. When read carefully, this book will produce a paradigm shift in how churches see family and adult ministries. **This is a landmark book for church leaders and grandparents alike.**

LARRY FOWLER
Founder, The Legacy Coalition and Author of *Rock-Solid Kids* and *Raising a Modern-Day Joseph*

Josh Mulvihill is a great pioneer in grandparenting ministry from whom I have learned much. This book will inform you, but more than that, it will bless you and challenge you. If you are up for a challenge and want a clearer understanding of what God thinks about grandparenting, **this book is a must read.**

CAVIN T. HARPER
Executive Director, The Christian Grandparent Network and Author of *Courageous Grandparenting*

I cannot think of a more practical, biblical, insightful tool for "soon to be" or "in full swing" grandparents than Josh Mulvihill's new book, *Biblical Grandparenting.* Based solidly on God's word, filled with *meaningful* research, laced with "I can apply that!" insights, this book can help YOU walk well, wisely and joyfully with your grandchildren—and their parents—in the years to come. Give yourself—and your grandchild—a powerful gift for their future by getting and reading this book!

JOHN TRENT, PH.D.
Gary D. Chapman Chair of Marriage and Family MInistry and Therapy, Moody Theological Seminary
Author of *The Blessing* and President, StrongFamilies.com

BIBLICAL
GRAND PARENTING

EXPLORING GOD'S DESIGN, CULTURE'S MESSAGES
AND DISCIPLE-MAKING METHODS TO
PASS FAITH TO FUTURE GENERATIONS

JOSH MULVIHILL

Produced by the Denzel Agency (www.denzel.org)
Cover and text design by Rob Williams

Biblical Grandparenting
Print ISBN 978-0-9982058-0-9
Kindle ISBN 978-0-9982058-1-6
EPUB ISBN 978-0-9982058-2-3

Printed in the United States of America

For permissions please contact:
Biblical Grandparenting
5720 Marsh Lake Road
Chaska, MN 55318

16 17 18 19 20 | 5 4 3 2 1

To my children, future grandchildren,
great grandchildren, and great great grandchildren.

May you set your hope in God

PSALM 78:5-7

Contents

Foreword

The church has assimilated the world's perspective on senior adult-hood and grandparenting—a perspective that sees senior adulthood as a sort of second adolescence, filled with maximal freedom and minimal responsibility. Like the wealthy fool in one of the parables of Jesus, many senior adults have declared to themselves, "You have plenty of goods stored up for many years; relax, eat, drink, celebrate!" (Luke 12:19). But Scripture calls older adults to something far more significant than sailing into the sunset on a ship that is free from responsibilities to the next generation. According to the apostle Paul, older believers are called to train and to encourage younger believers—a task that requires continuing growth and faithfulness in the local church (Titus 2:2-8).

This book is packed with solid biblical foundations and fresh empirical research. What Josh Mulvihill has provided here takes a significant step in the direction of developing a new vision for grandparents and senior adults in our churches. Read this work carefully, constantly seeking ways that your church might equip grandparents to be more effective as disciple-makers in the lives of their grandchildren and in the life of the local church.

Timothy Paul Jones, Ph.D.
C. Edwin Gheens Professor of Christian Family Ministry,
The Southern Baptist Theological Seminary

Introduction

I began a Ph.D. degree in family ministry with the intention of doing my dissertation on family worship. While progressing through my coursework, I noticed a large void in the field of family ministry and became convinced that families and the church would benefit from a clear explanation of God's design for grandparents. I spent four years studying grandparenthood in depth and the results of my study are contained in the pages that follow.

This book is titled *Biblical Grandparenting* because our understanding of grandparenting needs to be based on the Bible. The Bible is sufficient for all matters of life, including grandparenting (2 Pet 1:3). Sadly, few grandparents know what the Bible says on the subject. Most look to other sources. In fact, most Christian grandparents have absorbed a philosophy of grandparenting that reflects secular culture rather than Scripture.

Two important truths are foundational to this book: *God designed grandparenting; therefore, God gets to define the role of grandparents.* God created grandparents because he has an important purpose for them and he clearly communicates it to us in the Bible.

I wrote this book to encourage grandparents to pass on faith in Christ to future generations. With that in mind, I have three goals for this book: (1) to explain what the Bible says about grandparenting, (2) to summarize what American culture says about grandparenting, and (3) to equip you to be a disciple-making grandparent. I pray God uses this work for his glory and starts a movement of churches that take seriously God's role for grandparents as disciple-makers of the youngest generation.

Why Grandparenting?

Grandparenthood, in general, is misunderstood, unappreciated, and under-resourced. Grandparenting is not highly valued in America or in the church. Grandparents have an opportunity to make a significant spiritual impact, but are settling for an independent existence that does not interfere with their adult children's decisions and places them at the periphery of family life. Grandparents need a multigenerational, gospel-centered vision for their life. There are four reasons why a book on grandparenting is needed.

1. It's Biblical, Yet Misunderstood

There are hundreds of references to grandparents or grandparenting in the Bible. The central thrust of these Scripture passages is that God designed grandparents to be key disciple-making influences in the lives of children. God has a plan and a purpose for grandparents, which focuses on the transmission of faith in Christ to future generations. A grandparent, like a father and mother, is given a distinct role in the family that is different from all other adults in a child's life. Grandparents have a unique role that is irreplaceable and influential.

Grandparents are the adjunct servants of a godly parent and a spiritual surrogate for an ungodly parent. Grandparents are another voice meant to encourage children to embrace the gospel. Grandparents provide the counsel of godly wisdom and the example of a godly life. Grandparents are a stabilizing force in the family. They are a last line of defense when crisis hits and a built-in support system for the home. They offer affirmation and affection that is second only to parents in its impact on children. In short, the Bible presents grandparents as important and gives them an important role in the family.

2. Limited Resources

There are an estimated thirty million Christian grandparents in America today with few resources to equip them to accomplish the role God has given them in Scripture. At the time of my study, there were fewer than a dozen books, one DVD series, and one ministry that existed to support all thirty million Christian grandparents. You might think that this sounds like a lot of resources, but can you imagine only having a few books to address all the parenting needs for all Christian parents today? Christian grandparents are under-resourced from a Christian perspective on topics such as long-distance grandparenting, grandparents as parents, grandfatherhood, grandparenting a grandchild with a disability—and that is the tip of the iceberg. Like grandparents themselves, Christian grandparenting has been overlooked and undervalued, as reflected by the fact that pastors and publishers have almost completely ignored the subject.

Three resource providers are leading the way to encourage and equip grandparents to pass on faith in Christ to future generations:

- The Christian Grandparent Network led by Cavin Harper. Cavin is a pioneer in ministry to grandparents and has served this demographic for two decades. Cavin offers a number of wonderful resources such as his book *Courageous Grandparenting*, Grand-Camps, and a prayer focus in partnership with Lillian Penner who wrote *Grandparenting with a Purpose: Effective Ways to Pray for Your Grandchildren*.

- The Legacy Coalition led by Larry Fowler. Larry has a vision to start a national movement of intentional, Christ-centered grandparenting in America. The Legacy Coalition, a ministry of Awana, offers a national grandparenting conference and provides resources such as *Equipping Grandparents: Helping Your Church Reach and Disciple the Next Generation*.

- The National Association of Grandparenting led by Dr. Ken Canfield. Dr. Canfield offers research and resources to help grandparents succeed in their role. For a modest fee, you can join the association and receive a magazine, benefits, and other perks.

3. Limited Research

The majority of research on grandparenting does not address the spiritual component of the role. Prior to this study, limited research had been done on the biblical-theological facet of the grandparent's role and no research had been done on the role of grandparents in a Christian context. In the Ph.D. world, it is frowned upon to state that no one has written on a topic or that a subject has been untouched. However, the more I explored the topic of Christian grandparenting, the more I noticed how little research has been done on the subject.

It is my hope that Christian scholars build upon my work and continue to study the topic of Christian grandparenting. Grandparents may be the most under-researched demographic in family studies, providing ample research options as well as ensuring that research findings will be impactful, and in some cases even groundbreaking.

4. Grandparents are Influential

Who are the most influential people in a young person's life? A Barna study wanted to know the answer to a similar question and asked 602 teenagers, "Who, besides your parents, do you admire most as a role model?" According to Barna, the top five influences in the life of young people are: (1) parents, (2) other family members, typically grandparents, (3) teachers and coaches, (4) friends, and (5) pastors or religious leaders.[1]

After parents, grandparents are the greatest potential influence in the life of a child, not a peer, not a pastor, and not a teacher. Grandparents, you should be encouraged. Young people admire you. They believe you are an important person in their life.

When teenagers were asked why they named a particular person as influential, teens provided the following reasons: they were worthy of imitation, they wanted to follow in the footsteps of the chosen person, they were always there for the teenager, and they were interested in the teenager's future.

David Kinnaman, president of Barna Group, explains why grandparents have so much influence in a young person's life. "Notice that a majority of teens indicated the people they most admire and imitate are those with whom they maintain a personal connection, friendship, or interaction." Kinnaman continues, "For better and worse, teens are emulating the people they know best." As basic as it sounds, grandchildren typically imitate the people who spend the most time with them.

Do you want your grandchildren to follow Christ? According to this research, the first step is to develop a strong relationship that maintains an active presence in a grandchild's life. Grandparents who are emotionally distant and physically disengaged limit the influence they will have on the faith of grandchildren. If churches want to impact the faith of young people, strategically, the greatest return on investment will come from equipping parents and grandparents to be disciple-makers within their own families.

Overview of the Book

This book will prove helpful for grandparents and church leaders. It can be read individually or used in Sunday school classes, small groups, and college classes. Every Christian grandparent would benefit from knowing the biblical principles of grandparenting presented in this book.

I want you to know what to expect from this book. A professor told me that only two people will want to read my study: my mom and wife. Historically, dissertations do not generate high volume readership. However, I believe this book is different because the subject matter has been neglected for so long and a wake up call is needed. I want you to know that this book was written as an academic work. The style and language will reflect that. There will be hundreds of footnotes.

I added a chapter to the beginning of the dissertation written in a format that is easy to read. If you don't like reading scholarly material, then simply read the first chapter and use my dissertation as reference material, jumping around as desired. However, I encourage you to read the book in its entirety. If you do not, you will miss key findings, a deep dive into culture's messages, and the discipleship practices of effective Christian grandparents. Here are examples of key findings you might miss if you don't read the study in full:

- Three-quarters of the Christian grandparents I interviewed do not have a clear understanding of their role and operate closer to cultural norms than biblical imperatives. Grandparents are willing to invest spiritually in the lives of their grandchildren, but they are unsure what is expected of them. As a result, most Christian grandparents do not have an intentional plan to disciple future generations and lack a vision for how God can use them to impact their grandchildren with the gospel.

- An expanded definition of "family" is needed. The family, according to cultural definitions, consists of a parent(s) and children and is defined in nuclear terminology. The Bible defines family in extended family terminology, which includes grandparents. The Bible places expectations on how the generations are to interact and what responsibilities they have to one another. If a family consists only of parents and children, then grandparents are an extra, nonessential component of the family.

- I interviewed 25 different grandparents from 25 different churches across the country and asked each one what their church has done to equip them in their role as a grandparent. One church offered a seminar on grandparenting. Not a single sermon, Sunday school class, small group series, or grandparent ministry was present at any of these churches. Imagine if a church never addressed parenting or marriage. This is the current reality for grandparents. Churches have completely ignored the subject, which means grandparents are left to figure things out on their own without the support or guidance of their pastors.

- Grandparents struggle reading the Bible and verbally sharing the gospel with grandchildren. About half of the grandparents read a children's story Bible with their grandchildren, but once a grandchild grows out of this stage, the percentage of grandparents reading and discussing Scripture with grandchildren plummets to extremely low levels. In addition, only one in four grandparents had verbally shared the gospel with their grandchild stating that this was someone else's responsibility.

Part 1: Getting Started

Part one is an overview of the entire study. The high points are summarized and easy to read. This section provides a theology of grandparenting and a concise synthesis of what the Bible says about the subject. I believe the unifying concept from Old Testament to New Testament Scripture is the idea of grandparents building a godly heritage by being disciple-makers who pass on faith in Christ to future generations. I break down the theology of grandparenting into ten biblical themes and refer to them as God's design for grandparents. The ten biblical themes of grandparenthood point back to the idea of building a godly heritage through the discipleship of grandchildren.

Part 2: God's Design

Part two lays the groundwork for the study by introducing the problem and explaining the research project. This section returns to Scripture to explore the biblical terms used to describe grandparenting and provides an academic perspective on six biblical themes of grandparenting.

Part 3: Culture's Messages

Part three explores what literature says about the role of grandparents and provides a comprehensive summary of the past 50 years of research on the role of grandparents. If you want to know what the culture says about grandparenting, are interested in a brief history of grandparenting in America, or would like an introduction to the major studies on the role of grandparents, this is the section to read.

Part 4: Discipleship Methods

Part four contains the summary of 25 interviews with evangelical grandparents from across the country. You will read what grandparents believe their role to be and the spiritual practices they use to help grandchildren grow in their faith. This section provides practical ideas to disciple grandchildren, found in quotes from grandparents, and in key findings of my analysis.

Note

1. www.barna.org/barna-update/millennials/467-teen-role-models#.V6tVFjqdLzI

PART 1:

GETTING STARTED

CHAPTER 1

An Overview of Grandparenting

Ten Biblical Themes
Every Grandparent Should Know

Every member of the family is given a clear, God-ordained role in Scripture that is not interchangeable with other members of the family. Husbands are referenced as the head of the home and are to lovingly lead their family (Eph 5:23). Wives are given the role of helpmate and are to willingly follow their husband's leadership (Gen 2:18; Eph 5:22). Children are told to honor their parents through obedience (Exod 20:12; Eph 6:1).

If the Bible clearly defines the role of family members, is it possible that it also defines the role of grandparents? This question has been one of the focal points of my Ph.D. dissertation and multiple years of study. The Bible has hundreds of references that directly or indirectly speak to grandparenting. Phrases such as children's children, son's son, father's father, old age, and forefathers help us understand the place and purpose of grandparents in the home.

Although the Bible is clear about the role of grandparents, American culture is not and many Christians have unintentionally adopted this unbiblical view of grandparenthood. Generally speaking, in American culture there is confusion concerning the meaning and purpose of a grandparent's role. Gunhild Hagestad, author of *Grandparenting*, says, "There is new uncertainty about what it means to be a grandparent and what grandparents are supposed to do."[1]

Cultural Messages About Grandparenting

America has created its own role for grandparents, and that role is part of what is known to scholars as "the new social contract." The core values of this social contract include non-interference by grandparents, emotional independence from children, and personal autonomy. Families unconsciously operate according to the agreement that children will grow up, move away, start their own family, and become independent from one another. Experts encourage families to aim for closeness at a distance, but what they gain is lonely, overburdened, and disconnected families. This social contract has amputated generations from one another and left countless grandchildren as grand-orphans who do not have the intimate influence of a grandparent in their life.

Because the role of grandparents is not clearly defined by American culture, it is viewed as an extra, nonessential role to the functioning of the family or the growth and development of grandchildren. Grandparents themselves fear meddling in their children's and grandchildren's lives. While relationships that do exist can be very positive, their limited and tenuous nature removes grandparents from the central hub of family life and places them on the periphery with a minimal impact.

Over the past one hundred years society has redefined family with a focus on emotional companionship. One manifestation of this change is found in children's literature about grandparenthood. A few notable titles of children's books include *Grandmas Are for Giving Tickles* and *Grandpas Are for Finding Worms*. The children's book *What Grandpas and Grandmas Do Best* suggest that grandparents are for playing hide-and-seek, singing a lullaby, building a sandcastle, and playing games. In *Grandma, Grandpa, and Me* grandparents are to play with, work alongside, and have fun with. Children's literature speaks of a grandparent's role as playmate and companion.

Grandparents adjusted their value system based on the place and purpose society gave to the elderly and defined their involvement with family around the two roles of independence and indulgence. Values shifted from leaving a family legacy and financial inheritance to pursuing a pleasant retirement experience. A bumper sticker occasionally seen on the car of elderly people captures this well: "We're spending our children's inheritance."

Society has lost its compass regarding why the generations should interact, how to do so, and what responsibilities they have to the other. My research revealed that two out of three Christian grandparents operate according to three cultural guidelines: (1) adult children expect noninterference, (2) the primary role for grandparents is emotional-supportive, and (3) a high value is placed on encouragement and companionship. The majority of Christian grandparents interviewed for my study did not know what the Bible says about grandparenting. In fact, low numbers of grandparents referenced the Bible as they talked about their role. Christian grandparents need a renewed biblical vision regarding their role in the family and purpose in society.

God's Design for Grandparents

The Bible has much to say about the role of grandparents. During my year-long, cover-to-cover reading of the Bible, I cataloged every reference that applied to grandparents. At the end of that year, I had more than 100 pages of single-spaced notes and summarized them as God's design for grandparents broken down into 10 biblical themes. An overview can be seen in the chart below. Each theme speaks to a different component of God's design for grandparents. Together, they present a rich picture of a disciple-making role with a clear task of passing on faith in Jesus Christ to future generations.

Before exploring these 10 biblical themes, it is worth noting what the Bible does not say about the role of grandparents. The Bible never portrays a godly grandparent as self-focused, emphasizing fun as the goal with grandchildren, disconnected from the younger generations of their faith community, or living a separate life from their adult children and grandchildren. The Bible never encourages a season of retirement to travel or play. The Bible never endorses self-indulgence due to a lifetime of hard work. The Bible never encourages individual, autonomous lives between family generations.

Grandparents of the Bible were not bleacher-sitting, pleasure-seeking, purposefully-sedentary, second-class citizens. They were warriors (Caleb and Joshua), kings (David), prophets (Moses, Isaiah, Jeremiah, Anna), men or women of God (Noah, Lois), and apostles (John). They led churches and families. Grandparents of the Bible were active and impactful. Their lives were full, and, God willing, long. In God's economy, grandparents were essential; they were not optional. Their lives were Jesus-oriented, not self-indulgent.

Table 1. Ten biblical themes

Biblical Theme	Grandparent Responsibility
Grandparents have inherited a faith they are to pass on to their children and children's children (Deut 6:4-9, 12:28; Ps 71:16-18).	Build a legacy of faith by passing on biblical teachings, traditions, and faithfulness.
Grandparents are to leave an inheritance to future generations (Prov 13:22; Eccl 7:1).	Provide children and grandchildren with a financial inheritance and a name that is worthy of honor.
Grandchildren are desirable and a crowning glory in life (Ps 128:6; Prov 17:6).	Recognize the value of grandchildren. Grandchildren are a gift from God.
Grandparents are to be honored (Exod 20:12; Prov 23:22; 1 Tim 5:18).	Future generations have a responsibility to honor grandparents and care for them in their old age.
Grandparents who live in rebellion to God and do not walk in his ways may influence future generations to follow a similar path (2 Kgs 17:41; Ps 103:17; Deut 4:40; Exod 34:6-7).	Live in obedience to God and exhort future generations to do the same while warning them of the consequences of sin. Be a living story worthy of imitation.
Grandparents are to have a multigenerational vision for the salvation and sanctification of the family (Ps 78:1-8; 2 Tim 1:5).	Proclaim the gospel, point to Christ, and pray for future generations.
Grandparents are to utilize specific spiritual practices to pass on faith to future generations (Deut 4:9; Ps 78:1-8).	Build a godly heritage by teaching the truths of God's Word and retelling the story of God's work.
Old age, the season of grandparenthood, increases one's potential contribution to God and others (Gen 2:15; Ps 92:14-15; Prov 6:6-11; Deut 6:1-2).	Reject the narrative that the purpose of old age is a life of leisure and self-indulgence but rather to serve God and bear fruit until one's dying day.
Grandparents have a responsibility to the church, which includes the discipleship of younger men and women (Titus 2:1-6).	Older generations are to train younger generations by providing biblical wisdom, guidance, and instruction.
Old age is a sign of God's favor and something to celebrate (Ps 90:9-10; Prov 14:15).	Reject the cultural view of old age as undesirable, embrace old age, and live intentionally for Christ.

1. Heritage of Faith

The one word that summarizes a grandparent's role from a biblical standpoint is heritage (Ps 78:1-8; 62-63). Grandparents have inherited a faith they are to pass on to their children *and* their grandchildren (Deut 4:9; 6:1-2) In modern terminology, the word legacy is more commonly used to communicate a similar idea of passing on faith or finances to future generations. In the narrative of Scripture, grandparents can be observed passing on faith through biblical teachings, traditions, and by living a godly life in obedience to the Lord.

The grandparent's role is to leave a godly legacy and build a rich heritage in the Lord. To be clear, the grandparent is not building their own heritage, they are passing on the Lord's heritage. Psalm 127:3 says, "children (and thus, grandchildren) are a heritage from the Lord." Just as a child does not truly belong to a parent, so a heritage does not truly belong to a grandparent (Ps 24:1). The author of Proverbs 13:22 encourages grandparents to leave an inheritance for grandchildren, which has both financial and spiritual applications.

The Bible warns grandparents that disobedient and rebellious descendants are the result of spiritually neglecting the faith of children and grandchildren. God designed grandparents to be disciple-makers who treasure Christ, tell grandchildren the work of God, and teach grandchildren the truths of God's Word (Ps 78:4-8). Biblical grandparenting centers on discipleship, is a crowning achievement of life, and focuses on the salvation and sanctification of future generations. Consistently throughout Scripture, older generations are investing in younger generations.

The most common passage of Scripture utilized for family discipleship is Deuteronomy 6:4-9. Currently, the Christian community limits the application of Deuteronomy 6 to parents, but based on the context of Deuteronomy 6:1-2 it has a broader application that includes grandparents.

In Deuteronomy 5 and 6, Moses summoned all Israel, including grandparents, and gave the community a charge to love God and diligently teach young people the commands of God (Deut 5:1; 6:1-2). As you read the following verse, notice *who* is to be a recipient of the commands of God. Moses states, the commands of God are for "you and your son and your *son's son*" (Deut 6:1-2). The reference to "son's son" is one of the Bible's ways of saying "grandchildren" and suggests that Deuteronomy 6:4-9 is not only for children, but also for grandchildren.[2]

Grandparents as well as parents are given the responsibility by God, "You shall teach them diligently to your children" (Deut 6:7).[3] Grandparents have been given a God-designed role that includes teaching grandchildren the commands of God. If God desires to see tri-generational faithfulness, it makes sense that God will employ a multigenerational strategy utilizing parents and grandparents to accomplish his desired outcomes.

2. Inheritance

Grandparents are to leave an inheritance to future generations. Proverbs 13:22 says, "A good man leaves an inheritance to his children's children." According to the Bible, grandparents have something of value that God designed to be intentionally passed on to children and grandchildren. Grandparents are not to squander a family's inheritance on themselves.

The Bible speaks of multiple ways grandparents leave an inheritance to future generations: financial, a good name, and salvation. Proverbs 19:14 presents a norm in Scripture, "House and wealth are passed on from [grand]fathers." My interviews with Christian grandparents around the country showed that grandparents do not have a clear understanding or application of Proverbs 13:22. Christian grandparents operate according to four different approaches to handling finances in later life: (1) spend now on family, (2) spend now of self, (3) provide a spiritual inheritance, and (4) save for family. The prudent grandparent gives forethought to what he or she would like to pass on and makes a financial plan toward that end.

Grandparents will also pass on a name, which will either be a blessing or a curse to future generations. The author of Ecclesiastes says, "A good name is better than precious ointment" (Eccl 7:1). At the most basic level, grandparents pass on a reputation based on how they lived their life. Grandparents pass on a name of highest value when they walk with the Lord and live for God's glory. Grandparents are reminded by Ecclesiastes 7:1 that there is little value in expensive outward enjoyments such as perfumes. Based on eternity, to be a child of God and to have one's name confessed by Christ before the Father in heaven is better than all riches and the greatest inheritance a grandparent can pass on to a grandchild. Grandparents who wish to spoil their grandchildren should give grandchildren an inheritance that cannot spoil: a rich heritage in Christ.

3. The Gift of Grandchildren

Every grandchild is created in the image of God and is therefore a blessing of great worth to grandparents (Gen 1:28). Every grandchild, regardless of race, gender, health, disability, personality, or achievement, is to be highly valued. Grandchildren are a blessing not because of who they are or what they will do, but because they are created by God for his glory and as a good gift to grandparents. Every grandchild is to be received with open arms, even the most difficult or severely disabled grandchild.

The Bible tells us it is a blessing to know one's grandchildren. Psalm 128:6 says, "May you see your children's children!" Biblical grandparenting is embodied by enthusiasm, not ambivalence, about becoming a grandparent. Grandparents should treat the demands of being a grandparent not as a burden, but as a blessing. The grandparent who has a poor attitude toward grandparenthood in general or a grandchild specifically is at odds with God's sovereign plan. Grandparenting is to be embraced as God's good design for the later third of life, not avoided, abdicated, or considered a burden.

It is critical for grandparents to approach this season of life with an attitude toward grandchildren that reflects God's attitude. How does the Bible speak of grandchildren? Proverbs 17:6 says, "Grandchildren are a crown of the aged." God speaks about grandchildren as a crown, suggesting they are of high value and bestow upon grandparents an honor unmatched and unavailable through any other source. The attitudes and actions of Christian grandparents should reflect the value given to grandchildren by God in Scripture. Like any recipient of a gift, grandparents have the choice to receive or reject God's good gift of grandchildren. As we read through the narrative of Scripture, grandparents who receive grandchildren as a gift respond to them with warm affection.

Toward the end of his life, Jacob the patriarch called his grandsons to him to bless them; he "kissed them and embraced them" (Gen 48:10). Another example is seen in the life of Laban: "Early the next morning, Laban kissed his grandchildren and his daughters and blessed them" (Gen 31:55). If Laban, an ungodly man, knew the importance of affection, then grandparents who have been transformed by Christ should demonstrate an even greater affection. Naomi displayed a loving affection for her grandson: "Then Naomi took the child, laid him in her lap and cared for him" (Ruth 4:16). What a wonderful picture of grandparents at work! Every grandchild benefits from a grandparent who loves him or her outrageously. In an age when life is difficult, affection from a grandparent provides another source of safety and security for children. Even more important, strong relationships become the foundation by which the gospel can be transmitted and discipleship between generations can occur.

4. Honoring Grandparents

Numerous scholars speak of the centrality of the fifth commandment to the subject of grandparenting. A growing number of scholars believe that the command to honor one's parents was not directed only toward young children, but includes adult children for the purpose of caring for their aging family members.[4] Ronald Clements holds this position and says: "The whole aim of this commandment is to secure positive support for ageing [sic] parents from their children, who are themselves assumed to be mature parents.... It is this care of the old that is demanded here."[5] Donald Knight has the following to say:

> The commandment "Honor your father and your mother" (Exod 20:12) is not directed so much at young children as it is at adults who are obligated to care for their elderly parents. Similarly, the harsh law in Deuteronomy 21:18-21 does not prescribe capital punishment for a minor who disobeys his or her parents, for drunkenness and gluttony are most offensive when they result in an adult's shirking the responsibility of providing for the needs of one's parents. The biblical text makes it a moral and social duty, the violation of which is punishable by the community.[6]

Gordon Harris has a helpful summary of the fifth command. He says the word honor as "used here emphasizes the giving of 'weight' to prominent people. It commonly refers to glorifying God." Harris interprets this to mean that "children must grant full significance to parents" which includes "making them feel important for what they have achieved as parents and for what they have accomplished as the instructors of younger generations (Deut 6:7, 20-21)."[7]

Honoring one's parents includes applications for the aging, but should not be limited to this period of life.[8] Honoring parents is a command that applies to adult children and grandchildren alike. It is not an attitude only, but includes the element of personal service.[9] Honor is demonstrated by positive action on behalf of grandparents—meeting their needs, listening to their advice, recognizing their worth, and doing so in all sorts of ways large and small (1 Tim 5:1; Lev 19:32; Prov 23:22).[10] Dishonoring older family members through speech (Lev 20:9) or in deed (Exod 21:15; Prov 28:24) was a serious offense, further establishing the importance that Scripture places on honoring elders.[11] The older generations in Scripture are given a place of honor that is often absent from modern society.[12] The attitude of the younger generations toward grandparents should reflect God's attitude towards grandparents. In general, the Bible holds them in high esteem and suggests the later years of a person's life are "a time of divine tribute."[13]

The Bible illustrates a number of ways in which grandparents can be honored: devotion (Ruth 1:16); financial support, especially for widows (Acts 6:1-4; 1 Tim 5:3-8); providing a caring fellowship (Acts 2:42-26); and listening to their advice and wisdom (1 Tim 5:17-18). In Matthew 15:1-6, Jesus interprets the commandment, "Honor your father and mother," as referring to financial support. John MacArthur's pastoral perspective further explains this passage's meaning.

> The Old Testament law of honoring one's parents meant that as long as a person lived, he was to respect and support his parents. During the first half of a person's life, the parents give everything they have to supply the needs of their children. When they get to the point in life where they're no longer able to meet their own needs, it becomes the responsibility of their children to take care of them. That is God's way of making families stick together. The parents raise the children, and when the children are grown, they take care of their parents while also raising their own children, who are going to take care of them while they are raising their children.[14]

It is noteworthy that as important as parenting is in the Bible, a high honor is also reserved for grandparents.[15] God instructed those in the community of faith to "stand up before the gray head and honor the face of an old man, and you shall fear your God" (Lev 19:32).[16] In this passage, Moses links showing respect for the aged with having reverence for God.

Grandparents are honored when young people listen to their wisdom. Elihu, one of Job's friends, "had waited to speak to Job because they [three other friends] were older than he" (Job 32:4). Elihu purposefully acted with reverence toward those who were older. "I said, let days speak, and many years teach wisdom" (Job 32:7). Rehoboam is not presented in Scripture as a model for young people to follow. He rejected the counsel of old men in place of advice from the young, and it cost him the majority of his kingdom (1 Kgs 12:6-15). Job states, "Wisdom is with the aged, and understanding in length of days" (Job 12:12). Grandparents have accumulated wisdom, and wise grandchildren glean much from the aged.

Just as the older generation has a responsibility to spiritually nurture the younger generation, the younger generation has the responsibility to honor and care for the older generation. Honoring the older generation is the key responsibility of younger generations. It is the first command with a promise because it is the key to all human relationships and the passing on of a righteous heritage.

5. The Sin of Fathers

God never allows grandparents to sin successfully. The Bible says the sin of a father often becomes the sin of the family for multiple generations. One example is found in 2 Kings 17:41, "So these nations feared the Lord and also served their carved images. Their children did likewise, and their children's children—as their [fore]fathers did, so they do to this day." Grandparents who live in rebellion to God and do not walk in his ways may influence future generations to follow a similar path (Ps 103:17; Deut 4:40; Exod 34:6-7).

Grandchildren watch the lives of grandparents and regularly absorb a grandparent's priorities, passions, and perspectives. The multigenerational examples provided from Scripture are sobering. In Judges 2, Psalm 78, and the list of Kings, each generation gave themselves over to a greater degree of depravity. In each of these examples the move away from the Lord began slowly with a divided heart and ended with descendants that did not know the Lord or walk in his ways.

The first and most important command for all grandparents is to love the Lord with all their heart, soul, and might (Deut 6:4). A grandparent cannot properly disciple future generations if they have a competing love (know in Scripture as an idol). God's first concern is for a grandparent's heart, followed by daily discipleship practices with the family.

Grandparents, as with every other member of the family, are called to love the Lord Jesus with their whole heart (Mark 12:30-31), deny themselves, follow Christ (Matt 16:24), and forsake all that prevents them from taking hold of Christ (Matt 13:44-46). Scripture sounds a loud warning to grandparents when it states, "their fathers forgot my name" and "have not obeyed my words" (Jer 23:27; 25:8). To all Christians, grandparents included, are the words of Romans 6:12, "Let not sin therefore reign in your mortal body," and Colossians 1:10, "Walk in a manner worthy of the Lord, fully pleasing to him."

Grandparents are called to model godliness before grandchildren. Older Christians can model how to live for Christ in a sinful world and how to respond to suffering. "Numbering our days" (Ps 90:12) helps younger Christians determine to live out their days wisely. Grandparents can model a vibrant walk with the Lord before younger generations through prayer, praise, and lifelong service.

Grandparents who are serious about passing on faith to grandchildren must live in obedience to God and exhort future generations to do the same while warning them of the consequences of sin. Biblical grandparenting begins with a passionate love for God, which leads to obeying his commands, and powerfully impacts future generations to imitate the godly lifestyle of the grandparent. Grandparents should live in such a way that they are able to say to a grandchild, "Imitate me as I imitate Christ" (1 Cor 11:1).

6. A Multigenerational Vision

What is the biblical role of a grandparent? Psalm 78:4-8 answers this question as clearly and comprehensively as any passage in the Bible. In Psalm 78, Asaph combines a compelling vision with a somber warning to motivate the older generation to take seriously the role God has entrusted to them.

A critical element of a grandparent's role is to adopt a biblical vision for their family. Psalm 78:6-7 provides that vision: "that the next generation might know them, the children yet unborn, and arise and tell them to their children, so that they should set their hope in God and not forget the works of God, but keep his commandments." Grandparents are given a four-generation vision, which equates to 150 years, and are instructed to diligently work towards two goals: the salvation and sanctification of future generations.

This passage discredits the mindset that a parent's job is complete when children grow up and leave the house. According to Psalm 78, a parent's job is never finished. Rather, it expands to include future generations. In this passage, four generations are referenced: the reader, the next generation, children yet unborn, and their children. Parents are exhorted to care deeply for the future spiritual state of all these generations, not just their immediate family. Grandparents are given a four-generation vision for the salvation and sanctification of their family and this reality should be reflected in a grandparent's priorities and passions.

7. Tell of God's Works and Teach God's Words

At the center of Asaph's vision for family discipleship in Psalm 78 are the two goals for every grandparent. Biblical grandparents are to encourage future generations to place hope in God (salvation) and keep his commandments (sanctification). Faithful grandparenting consists of focusing one's energy and efforts on these two areas. Thus, it is insufficient for the goal of grandparenting to be happy or healthy grandchildren, grandchildren who are well behaved or well educated, a grandparenting role that affirms but does not exhort, or supports but does not instruct. Each of these outcomes falls short of God's vision if they are disconnected from the two goals of salvation and sanctification of grandchildren.

Psalm 78 presents not only the goal of grandparenting, but also how to accomplish this God-sized vision. Grandparents are to busy themselves with two activities: telling and teaching. A key element of every grandparent's role is to tell grandchildren about the work of God and is found in Psalm 78:4, which says, "We will not hide them from their children, but tell to the coming generation the glorious deeds of the Lord, and his might, and the wonders he has done." In Hebrew, "to tell" means to report, to count, to make known, to make a written record.

God is very specific about the content he wants grandparents to discuss with grandchildren. Telling recounts, as a testimony, one's experience with God, what God has done, and who God is. Grandparents can use life lessons and tell stories to intentionally magnify the nature and person of God in the hearts of grandchildren. Just as God has established a testimony in Jacob, he has also established a testimony in every grandparent (Ps 78:5). God expects grandparents to share, in the form of testimony, the work of God in their lives, which could include times of God's provision, God's faithfulness, and their conversion.

Psalm 145:4-12 and Psalm 71:15-18 are two additional passages that provide a glimpse into the types of discussions every grandparent should have with their grandchildren. Psalm 145:4 says, "One generation shall commend your works to another, and shall declare your mighty acts." In short, grandparents are to remind the younger generation who God is and what he has done, using their own life experience.

According to Psalm 78, the role of a grandparent centers on teaching grandchildren the commandments of God. In Psalm 78:5 we read, "He appointed a law in Israel, which he commanded our fathers to teach their children." Biblically, we are reminded that grandparents share in the faith training of future generations and should actively invest in a grandchild's discipleship through teaching the Scriptures. It is important to note that God commands grandparents to teach grandchildren his commandments. Teaching is not optional. The grandparent who neglects this aspect of his or her role does so in disobedience to God.

In case you are unconvinced by Psalm 78, I will point you to Deuteronomy 4:9 which instructs grandparents to "teach [God's commands] to your children and your children's children." Theologians, such as Roy B. Zuck, believe grandparents have a teaching responsibility with grandchildren, "Teaching the young God's ways is a responsibility assigned not only to parents, but also to grandparents."[17]

To teach (ידע yada) is to instruct or guide for the purpose of learning.[18] What are grandparents to teach grandchildren? God has given grandparents the role of teaching core biblical truths, sound doctrine, and God's commands to grandchildren. In addition, grandparents are to instruct their grandchildren to walk obediently before the Lord and fear him all the days of their lives (Deut 4:10; 14). Grandparents teach for the purpose of seeing their grandchildren mature in Christ. The apostle Paul says, "Him we proclaim, warning everyone and teaching everyone with all wisdom, that we may present everyone mature in Christ. For this I toil, struggling with all his energy that he powerfully works within me" (Col 1:28-29).

One grandparent who is worthy of closer examination is Lois. Lois was the grandmother to Timothy and played an important role in the development of his spiritual life (2 Tim 1:5). The apostle Paul suggests that Lois taught Timothy the Scriptures from an early age, which became foundational in his following Christ (2 Tim 3:14-15). Lois' example, while not prescriptive for every grandparent, is worthy of imitation. Grandparents might consider three principles for teaching grandchildren from the life of Lois:

1. Early instruction (2 Tim 1:5; 3:15)
2. Frequent instruction (2 Tim 3:14)
3. Jesus-centered instruction (2 Tim 3:15)

In addition to the example of Lois, grandparents may glean from other biblical methods of teaching younger generations the truths of God's word. Throughout the narrative of Scripture we see older generations build traditions into their family life that remind younger generations of the salvation of the Lord.[19] Home décor, food, clothing, and stone pillars were all utilized to create discussion between young and old regarding the work and nature of God. Grandparents may choose to intentionally put items in their home that evoke curiosity, invite questions, and create the opportunity to teach the truths of Scripture to grandchildren.

In addition to the compelling vision of Psalm 78, grandparents are given a sober warning to avoid grandchildren becoming "like their fathers, a stubborn and rebellious generation, a generation whose heart was not steadfast, whose spirit was not faithful to God." Psalm 78:9-72 recounts the sad history of Israel's failure to transfer faith from the older generations to the younger generations, resulting in rebellion and unbelief. Phrases such as "they sinned still more against him," "they did not believe in God," and "they tested God again and again" remind today's grandparents that history may repeat itself if they neglect to transfer faith to future generations.

Grandparents are given an important, God-ordained role that makes an eternal difference in the lives of grandchildren. Psalm 78 reminds grandparents that they have a strong influence on the faith of grandchildren and provides grandparents with a God-centered picture regarding how they are to interact with grandchildren. It also provides the goal of grandparenthood and two tasks that are central to the role of grandparenting: telling the story of God's works and teaching the truths of God's Word.

8. Continued Fruitfulness in Old Age

The psalmist teaches that righteousness in old age results in the continued production of spiritual fruit. The psalmist uses the picture of a palm tree to make his point: "The righteous will flourish like a palm tree, they will grow like a cedar of Lebanon; planted in the house of the Lord, they will flourish in the courts of our Lord. They will still bear fruit in old age, they will stay fresh and green, to declare that the Lord is upright; he is my rock, and there is no unrighteousness in him" (Ps 92:12-14).

Date palm trees bear hundreds of pounds of fruit well past 150 years of age and are a picture of what God expects from grandparents in the later third of their life. Whether referencing a palm tree or a grandparent, God expects continued fruitfulness for the purpose of declaring the nature of God to others.

Psalm 92 shouts a truth that all grandparents need to hear: age does not impair fruit-bearing capabilities. It enhances them. Psalm 92 reminds grandparents of two important truths. First, the latter years of a person's life ought to be spiritually productive years. American culture attempts to convince grandparents that they have little to offer. Nothing is further from the truth. Second, this passage speaks against the American ethos of retirement and reminds grandparents to be fruitful disciple-makers to their dying day. Ruth and Elmer Towns encourage retired individuals to have an eternal mindset when thinking about retirement. "What is retirement for ... shuffleboard ... fishing ... puttering around the house? While all these things are enjoyable, nothing is more eternal than investing your time and wisdom in a grandchild."[20]

Grandparents need to reject the narrative that the purpose of old age is a life of leisure and self-indulgence. The example of the palm tree suggests that a fruitless existence is not a category the Bible recognizes. God's expectation for palm trees is also true for grandparents: to live is to bear fruit, even in one's old age. Let every grandparent remember that God does not give senior discounts nor does he have retirement homes. One day, every grandparent will stand before Jesus Christ and will give an account for how they used the final third of their life. What kind of life lived would cause Jesus to say to a grandparent, "Well done, good and faithful servant"? According to Psalm 92, it is the fruitful grandparent.

9. Discipleship of Younger Christians

Grandparents have a responsibility to the church, which includes the discipleship of younger men and women. According to Titus 2, older men are to invest in younger men and older women are to mentor younger women. The pattern Paul presents is one in which the older generations are to train younger generations by providing biblical wisdom, guidance, and instruction.

The pattern presented in Titus 2, older Christians discipling younger Christians, is not the pattern for the majority of Christian grandparents interviewed in my study. In contrast to Titus 2, the average Christian grandparent is not directly involved with the youngest generation of their church in any meaningful way. The majority of grandparents have limited interaction with the young people of their congregation that amounts to a passing greeting in the hall and results in limited spiritual investment in their lives.

Grandparents stated two reasons why they no longer disciple the younger generation of their church. First, some grandparents believe they are unwanted, unneeded, or no longer able to offer something of value to young people. Second, other Christian grandparents believe they served their time and now it is someone else's turn.

In Titus 2, Paul gives an important leadership responsibility to the older generation, which centers on the discipleship of younger Christians. Biblical grandparents are models of the Christian life and teachers of younger generations. The church is in need of godly, mature Christians who will pour themselves into the lives of younger Christians.

10. Celebrate Old Age

The Bible says old age is a sign of God's favor and something to celebrate. Taking their cue from Scripture, grandparents should reject the cultural view of old age as undesirable and embrace this season of life with intentionality for Christ.

It is good to recognize that the Bible does not hide the negative side of growing older (2 Sam 19:34-35; 1 Kgs 1:1; 14:4; 15:23).[21] One of the most candid descriptions of what will happen to the grandparent's body in old age is provided in Ecclesiastes 12:1-7.[22] The elderly, Solomon says, lose their eyesight (v. 2), are bent over and shake (v. 3), have few teeth and lose hearing (v. 3), are fearful of others (v. 5), have limited sexual desire (v. 5), and are not far from death (v. 7).[23] According to Solomon, this is not the ideal time to begin serving the Lord, due to the physical limitations of this time of life.[24] Grandparents are exhorted not to squander the evening of their life in self-indulgent pursuits, nor waste any of the precious days that the Lord has given them, but to live for God's purposes rather than their own.

The Scriptures suggest that grandparents are not to spend their time thinking about their ailments or what they cannot do.[25] Even though the body weakens, God has promised, "Even to your old age I am he, and to gray hairs I will carry you. I have made, and I will bear; I will carry and will save" (Isa 46:4). The psalmist wrote, "My flesh and my heart may fail, but God is the strength of my heart and my portion forever."[26] Instead, grandparents should focus their eyes on God and his strength.

Grandparents are told by American culture that old age lies in wait, ready to steal one's youth.[27] Medications, creams, and surgeries are encouraged as protection against the danger of old age. One author summarizes America's obsession with looking young when he says,

Every morning across America, people peer into bathroom mirrors, searching for signs of age. No line, no blemish is overlooked. We dread the appearance of those little lines at the corners of our mouths and eyes, and then we console ourselves with the thought that, really, they are hardly noticeable. Still we know the truth. We are getting older—every day one day older. Rarely do we set aside our insecurities long enough to ask, "What are wrinkles? Where do they come from and what do they really mean?" Perhaps if we understood them better, we might fear them less.[28]

A society that panics people into painful Botox injections and disfiguring surgeries needs to be reminded that the Bible has a radically different view of old age. According to the Bible, gray hair and wrinkles are a crown and an honor.[29] The Bible welcomes old age; it does not try to protect against or reverse aging once it has begun. Gray hair is not to be despised, but appreciated as a sign of wisdom.[30] Wrinkles are not to be scorned, but valued as a sign of God's gift of long life. Proverbs 20:29 reminds grandparents that "the beauty of old men is their gray hair." Grandparents should embrace old age as a gift from God as it allows the grandparent to be a continued blessing to others.

Conclusion

Grandparents have a multifaceted and important role in the transfer of faith from one generation to the next. God has given grandparents a ministry of first importance with grandchildren. Absent from Scripture is any form of self-indulgent lifestyle. Grandparents must see their role as much more than being a fill-in-the-gaps, last line of defense, extra-special babysitter who dispenses large amounts of sugar. Rather, grandparents are essential components in God's plan to nurture the faith of future generations and they need to embrace the biblical role that God has given them.

Grandparents have a God-ordained purpose clearly defined in Scripture. The great purpose God has set before a grandparent is clear: teach the things of God "to your children and to your grandchildren" (Deut 4:9). Grandparents must live the gospel and speak of it so that generations to come might know Jesus Christ (Ps 78:1-8). Grandparents can encourage parents in their task, pray for the coming generations, pass on wisdom gleaned throughout life (Titus 2:1-5), stand in the gap when parents falter, and do so because their grand purpose is to pass on a heritage of faith and see grandchildren won to Christ.

When grandparents neglect to treasure Christ (Deut 6:1-2; 5) as well as teach the truth of God's words and tell wonders of God's work (Ps 78:4-7), a critical voice is silenced and grandchildren are more likely to struggle in their faith and walk away from the Lord.

I encourage you to take your cues regarding the role of grandparenthood from the Bible and not from culture. A grandparent's main role is not to spoil grandchildren or be their companion. A grandparent's purpose is not to indulge themselves during the last third of life. God has given grandparents the role of transferring faith to future generations. May you give yourself fully to this task so your grandchildren will be able to say with the psalmist, "We have heard with our ears, our [grand]fathers have told us, what deeds you performed in their days, in the days of old" (Ps 44:1).

Notes

1. Gunhild O. Hagestad, "Continuity and Connectedness," in *Grandparenthood*, ed. V. Bengtson and J. Robertson (Beverly Hills: Sage, 1985), 33.

2. Allen and Ross agree with this assessment, stating that, "Though these verses have often been assumed to be speaking exclusively to parents, these words convey the communal sense that faith in God is to be modeled and taught in the home as well as among the faith community, across the generations. Parents, grandparents, and all extended family ... are to participate in the telling of God's faithfulness to those coming along behind them." Holly Catterton Allen and Christine Lawton Ross, *Intergenerational Christian Formation* (Downers Grove: InterVarsity Press, 2012), 80.

3. The Bible's use of the words "son" and "children" in Deuteronomy 6:1-9 should be understood in a broader sense, allowing for grandchildren to be included in Moses' command, rather than a narrow sense and an application only to children. According to Francis Brown, the Hebrew word for son (בֵּן *bēn*) is primarily used for a male heir, one generation removed from a parent, but is also used to refer to grandchildren (see Exod 10:2; Judg 8:22; Jer 27:7; Exod 34:7; Deut 4:9, 25; Judg 12:14; 2 Kgs 17:41; 1 Chr 8:40; Job 42:16; Prov 13:22; 17:6; Ezek 37:25.) For example, Laban called his daughters' children his own sons (Gen 31:28, 43). Joseph called his grandchildren his sons (Gen 50:23). When a grandchild was born to Naomi, "the women of the neighborhood gave him a name, saying 'A son has been born to Naomi" (Ruth 4:17). The Bible uses the word son to include grandson, and is additional evidence that grandparents can claim Deuteronomy 6:4-9 as applicable to them. Francis Brown, S.R. Driver, and Charles A. Briggs, *Enhanced Brown-Driver-Briggs Hebrew and English Lexicon*, electronic ed. (Oak Harbor: Logos Research Systems, 2000), 119-120.

4. See Rolf Knierim, "Age and Aging in the Old Testament," in *Ministry with the Aging: Designs, Challenges, Foundations*, ed. William Clements (New York: Harper & Row, 1981), 29.

5. Ronald Clements, *Exodus*, The Cambridge Bible Commentary (London: Cambridge University Press, 1972), 125.

6. Douglas A. Knight, "Perspectives on Aging and the Elderly in the Hebrew Bible," *Interpretation: A Journal of Bible and Theology* 68, no. 2 (2014): 148.

7. J. Gordon Harris, *Biblical Perspectives on Aging: God and the Elderly* (New York: Haworth, 2008), 106.

8. Steven Sapp points out that the use of the word "obey" gives the commandment a much broader meaning, which includes application for young children. Steven Sapp, *Full of Years: Aging and the Elderly in the Bible and Today* (Nashville: Abingdon, 1987), 83.

9. Gerald Blidstein, *Honor Thy Father and Mother* (New York: KTAV Publishing House, 1975), 60-61.

10. Douglas K. Stuart, *Exodus*, New American Commentary, vol. 2 (Nashville: B & H, 2006), 461.

11. Sapp, *Full of Years*, 88.

12. Georges Minois recognizes this reality when he states, "Old people seem to have been genuinely respected, cosseted and obeyed in a general way; they benefited from a semi-religious prestige. Their fate would be envied by future generations." Georges Minois, *History of Old Age* (Chicago: University of Chicago Press, 1989), 30.

13. James Davies, "A Practical Theology of Aging: Biblical Perspectives for Individuals and the Church," *CEJ* 5, no. 2 (2008): 277.

14. John F. MacArthur, *The Fulfilled Family* (Chicago: Moody Press, 1981), 4.

15. Peter Enns sees an application of the fifth command extending to others in authority in the community. He states: "Many have suggested over the long history of interpretation that honoring 'your father and mother' necessarily extends to other people of authority in the community. This seems somewhat justifiable in light of the fact that the titles 'father' and 'mother' were applied to individuals other than parents (e.g., Judg 5:7; 1 Sam 24:11; 2 Kgs 5:13). Peter Enns, *Exodus*, The NIV Application Commentary (Grand Rapids: Zondervan, 2000), 420.

16. R. Laird Harris notes that "Verse 32 seems to be unique in the Pentateuch, though it is implied in the fifth commandment that honor be given to parents. Proverbs 20:29 and 16:31 give similar thoughts." R. Laird Harris, *Leviticus*, The Expositor's Bible Commentary, ed. Frank E. Gaebelein (Grand Rapids: Zondervan, 1990), 609.

17. Roy B. Zuck, *Precious in His Sight: Childhood & Children in the Bible* (Grand Rapids: Baker, 1996), 103.

18. Robert L. Thomas, New American Standard Hebrew-Aramaic and Greek Dictionaries: Updated Edition (Anaheim: Foundation Publications, Inc., 1998).

19. For a helpful book with many practical ideas see Noel Piper, *Treasuring God in Our Traditions* (Wheaton: Crossway, 2007).

20. Ruth Towns and Elmer Towns, "Grandparents in the Bible: What They Can Teach Us about Influencing Children," 42, emphasis original, accessed February 11, 2014, http://elmertowns.com/wp-content/uploads/2014/01/GrandparentsoftheBible.pdf. The book has been renamed *Great Lessons and Grand Blessings: Discover How Grandparents Can Inspire and Transform Their Grandchildren*.

21. For a quick overview see Harris, *Biblical Perspectives on Aging*, 84-90.

22. Scholars have suggested a variety of meanings for this passage ranging from literal, allegorical, to symbolic. On this range of meanings see Michael V. Fox, "Aging and Death in Qohelet 12," *Journal for the Study of the Old Testament* 42 (1988): 55-77.

23. For a more thorough explanation see Trevor H. Howell, "King Solomon's Portrait of Old Age," *Age and Aging* 16, no. 5 (1987): 331-333.

24. Paul Wegner, commenting on Ecclesiastes 12 states: "The preacher in the book of Ecclesiastes presents a graphic picture of the debilitating conditions common to 'old age,' but even he uses it to remind the reader to remember God before it is too late." Paul D. Wegner, "Old Age," in *New International Dictionary of Theology and Exegesis*, ed. Willem A. VanGemeren (Grand Rapids: Zondervan, 1997), 1:1136.

25. For a theological perspective on what one can expect in aging see Edward M. Andrews, "Finding Peace in Successful Aging," *New Theological Review* 23, no. 4 (2010): 13-20.

26. In Romans, the apostle Paul says that our bodies groan due to sin. Paul, speaking of the wonderful glory of our eternal home, provides comfort for those whose bodies are wasting away and reminds the Corinthians that the body is a temporary home (2 Cor 4:16; 5:1).

27. Michael Harrington's comments warrant hearing: "Perhaps the most important thing that must be done with regard to the aged is to change our operative philosophy about them. We have ... a 'storage bin' philosophy about them. We 'maintain' the aged; we give them the gift of life, but we take away the possibility of dignity. Perhaps one of the most basic reasons why America has such problems with its elderly men and women is that America really doesn't care about them. Michael Harrington, *The Older America: Poverty in the United States* (Baltimore: Penguin Books, 1962), 118.

28. William H. Thomas, *What Are Old People For? How Elders Will Save the World* (Acton, MA: VanderWyk & Burnham, 2004), 4.

29. vanThanh Nguyen, "Biblical Perspectives on Caring for the Aged and the Sick," *New Theology Review* 23, no. 4 (2010): 8.

30. Tremper Longman states: "Here modern Western society is out of odds with ancient Near Eastern and specifically biblical ideas. Today gray hair is something to be ashamed of. Youth now is venerated, but in antiquity gray hair, indicating advanced age, was a sign of distinction. The reason that age was respected was that, all things being equal, it meant that a person had matured and was wiser than a youth." Tremper Longman III, *Proverbs*, The Baker Commentary on the Old Testament Wisdom and Psalms (Grand Rapids: Baker, 2006), 386.

PART 2:

GOD'S DESIGN

CHAPTER 2

An Identity Crisis in America

Rejecting a Leisureville Lifestyle

The present research concern was driven by the desire to see grandparents more active in the spiritual formation of their grandchildren. Christian grandparents appear to have limited biblical knowledge regarding their role in the family[1] and are therefore delinquent at the task of training future generations to know and love Christ.[2] John Piper, recognizing this trend, states, "We are a self-centered generation [with] sights on a 'Sabbath evening' of life—resting, playing, traveling. . . . The mindset of our peers is that we must reward ourselves now in this life for the long years of our labor."[3] Could it be that Christian grandparents have been influenced by a cultural view of grandparenthood and have resigned themselves to a marginalized role characterized by ambivalence[4] toward their family's spiritual state and are primarily concerned with being an indulgent figure in their grandchild's life?[5] If true, these statements reveal both a large problem that exists in the Christian practice of family discipleship and a great opportunity for the academy to prepare pastors, parents, and grandparents to embrace and execute a greater vision for the household discipleship process. The concern, then, is that Christian grandparents are implementing an unbiblical approach to grandparenthood while abdicating their role as a disciple-making leader to their family.

Introduction to the Problem

Grandparents face an identity crisis in America.[6] Christian grandparents, taking their cues from culture, share society's confusion regarding their role in the family and responsibility to younger generations. Speaking of older adults in society, Arthur Kornhaber writes, "The result [of longer life] is general confusion about what we are to do with our extra years. . . . Meaningful roles and interests must be found."[7] In general, society has lost its compass regarding why the generations should interact, how they are to do so, and what responsibility one has to the other. Historically, grandparents have held a meaningful and important place in the family.[8] However, that place changed as the Industrial Revolution displaced families and rising divorce rates fragmented them, thereby altering the family landscape in America.[9]

Changes to family structure and grandparent function have become firmly embedded in American society while the current influence and role of grandparents in the life of families has not been studied in great detail.[10] An analysis of publications shows that only thirty-one books and scientific articles mentioning grandparents or grandchildren were published before 1984.[11] The limited amount of research focusing on grandparenthood explored topics such as the role of grandparents[12] and the meaning of grandparenthood[13] with a heavy emphasis on surrogate grandparents (grandparents raising grandchildren). In the past three decades there has been growing interest in grandparenthood and a rich database of research has emerged,[14] but in general there has been an absence of focus on the roles and relationships between intergenerational members of the family in the field of family studies. Arthur Kornhaber addresses the problem when he asks,

> Why had so little been written about grandparenting? Why was this important relationship all but ignored by my profession? . . . Indeed, grandparents were treated as if they didn't exist. I wondered why the mental health professionals traditionally viewed the family in a "nuclear" form—parents and children amputated from grandparent—when the family represents a multigenerational, biological, and social continuum? Didn't nature supply each child with six biological antecedents (two parents and four grandparents)? How did these people affect the growth and development of children? And why wasn't grandparenting being more intensively explored by professionals?[15]

The US population demographic growing most quickly is those over the age of sixty-five.[16] They represent more than a quarter of the entire US population, seventy-eight million in total.[17] Approximately 7,918 people turn sixty-two each day.[18] Since the beginning of the twentieth century, the number of Americans over the age of sixty-five has tripled; average life expectancy has risen from forty-seven to seventy-eight years.[19] Today, over 90 percent of Americans can expect to live past the age of sixty-five and most of these older adults will become grandparents.[20]

What is the church doing to care for and equip this growing population? One author believes, "As America rides the crest of an 'age wave,' the church is less than prepared for the impact of its thunderous crash upon culture."[21] Sociologists are committed to interpreting the implications of this "age wave." Christian educators would be wise to place a greater emphasis on this segment of the population and study the impact on the spiritual formation of the family and church. Baby Boomers (those born between 1946 and 1964) are members of what sociologists call the "lead generation."[22] A lead generation tends to set the agenda for the nation and for the church. This generation cannot be ignored, yet there is a need for a greater understanding of the cultural messages communicated to grandparents as well as the biblical foundations necessary to equip millions of grandparents to disciple their children and grandchildren.

The Primary Concern

In scholarly literature, the religious/spiritual facet of the grandparent-grandchild relationship has been neglected.[23] Research of this topic is limited to the sociological and psychological arenas and is almost nonexistent in the pastoral-theological perspective.[24] King, Burgess, Akinyela, Counts-Spriggs, and Parker note this omission: "Few empirical studies of grandparenting address religion."[25] Holly Catterton Allen notes that many of the largest and most respected studies on grandparents do not address religious issues or, at most, only briefly touch on the subject.[26] A number of theological questions have begun to be explored in greater depth such as, "What theological issues confront grandparents?" "Are there any theological implications concerning the increase in numbers of grandparents raising grandchildren?"[27] and, "Do grandparents influence their grandchildren spiritually?" "If so, how?"[28]

A handful of studies exist from a non-religious perspective on grandparent roles, yet there is limited research from a Christian perspective.[29] The spiritual dimension of a grandparent's role is absent from prior studies and, as a result, these studies prove to be only semi-useful for Christian grandparents who wish to understand their role as a spiritual presence in their grandchild's life.

A primary concern for family discipleship raised by scholars and theologians is that the family has failed to rise to the privilege and responsibility of passing the torch of faithfulness from one generation to the next.[30] This appears not only to be true of parents but of grandparents as well. According to Scripture, grandparents have a vital role in the transfer of faith from one generation to another.[31] Church and family culture have slowly minimized the role of grandparents as important spiritual leaders in their grandchild's life. Churches have segmented the generations from one another[32] and many families expect grandparents to indulge a grandchild with gifts rather than be a disciple-making influence in the grandchild's life. Research indicates that grandparents play an increasingly important role in the lives of their grandchildren.[33] Yet despite these findings there appears to be role confusion, high levels of ambivalence, and limited discipleship occurring from the oldest to the youngest generations.

A Case in Point

Andrew Blechman, author of *Leisureville*, explored what life is like as a retired person living in The Villages, a gated community in Florida. The Villages is larger than Manhattan, boasts a population over 100,000, has a golf course for every day of the month; and has its own newspaper, radio, and TV station. The Villages is missing only one thing: children. The Villages not only encouraged but legalized the segregation of ages from one another. No one under the age of nineteen may live there. Children may visit, but their stay is strictly limited to a total of thirty days a year.[34] When Dave, one of the residents, was asked if he was uncomfortable living in a community without children, he answered, "I'm not thirteen . . . I want to spend time with people who are my own age."[35] Another resident says, "I raised my children and I didn't want to raise anyone else's."[36] These residents have an appreciation for a new and growing phenomenon in American culture: age segregation.

The impact of age segregation on communities, families, and churches is significant. Blechman notes the negative impact the departure of his neighbors to The Villages will have on his community:

> Were the Andersons really going to drop out of our community, move to Florida, and sequester themselves in a gated geritopia? Dave and Betsy had volunteered on the EMS squad, and Betsy also volunteered at the senior center and our local hospice. By all accounts, they were solid citizens with many more years of significant community involvement ahead of them. And frankly, our community needed the Andersons. . . . Rather than lead, they had chosen to secede.[37]

The residents of The Villages do not attempt to conceal the fact that "at The Villages we spend our dollars on ourselves" and do not have to think about the 'problems' of our former communities and distant families.[38] One resident states, "The only thing I worry about these days is my daily golf game."[39] A carefree lifestyle dominated by leisure pursuits and warm weather is the driving priority for many who live in The Villages. There is a noticeable ambivalence toward future generations and a declining rate of volunteerism among this group.[40]

The self-indulgent values of many who live in The Villages are not isolated to this one group but reflect the society's views of retirement and role of the elderly in America. Retirement communities such as The Villages are so prevalent that the American Association of Retirement Communities (AARC) was created to encourage the formation of more retirement communities, support those that exist, and equip management to oversee them.[41]

Retirement is a recent phenomenon and the effects of this sociological revolution are just beginning to be understood.[42] For thousands of years, humans would work until they could not; but the growing prosperity of the last century made work optional for many in the later years of life. Throughout history, extended families lived together because survival required a collective effort.

A major sociological change, the formation of Social Security, unintentionally fueled the creation of a whole new class of people: retirees.

The combination of economic stability, retirement plans, and Social Security fueled a new period of life. Older Americans did not just retire from work; they retired from community and family, and began living a second adolescence characterized by limited responsibility and high levels of freedom.[43]

This new phase of life created an identity crisis in which older Americans began to ask what retirement was supposed to look like and what they were supposed to do with the remaining years they had left to live. Del Webb, a wealthy Arizonan entrepreneur, helped to redefine the role and place of the elderly in American society. In 1962, *Time Magazine* put Webb on the cover with the title, "The Retirement City: A New Way of Life for the Old."[44] Webb's research suggested that retirees would welcome the opportunity to distance themselves from their families and limit involvement; something once thought impossible. Webb built one of the first retirement communities and located it in Arizona, promising sunshine, low-cost living, and something to do. Webb sold this lifestyle as the new American Dream suggesting retirees "had worked hard, and now it was time to pursue hobbies, play golf, and socialize with their peers."[45] In 1962, the idea was so revolutionary, that *Time* made Webb its "Man of the Year." Webb had created a new national template for retirement in America that enticed older adults to relocate geographically far away from families and focus solely on themselves.

It is likely that many Christian grandparents have embraced the *Leisureville* mentality and need a renewed biblical vision regarding their role in the family and purpose in society. This research significantly contributes to the present literature as it describes the role given to grandparents by American society and demonstrates how Christian grandparents view their role and responsibility toward future generations.

Research Purpose

The purpose of this two-phase study is to provide a portrait of grandparenting from the Bible, an analysis of grandparenthood in American society, and discover the roles under which Christian grandparents currently operate. This research seeks to encourage families to embrace multigenerational discipleship and fill a gap in Christian education literature where limited emphasis has been placed. The potential contribution of this research is significant as it is appears that evangelical Christians have been greatly influenced by culture, are marginalized by family and church, confused about their role as grandparents, and resigned to minimal spiritual impact in their grandchild's life. Limited scholarly study on the roles of grandparents in evangelical contexts exists; the majority of popular resources available to encourage and equip Christian grandparents emphasize methodology while being weak in theology.[46] The present study addresses the spiritual responsibility of the grandparent toward grandchild and identifies the perceived roles grandparents utilize as they interact with their grandchildren. This research utilized a text-based approach of the Bible and sociological literature to analyze the role of grandparents and employed qualitative methods to gain a greater understanding of grandparents' perceived roles and accompanying practices.

Limitations of Research

The research was limited to familial grandparenthood, not spiritual grandparenthood, as defined by the literature and me. Because the purpose of this research was to discover the roles under which grandparents in evangelical contexts operate, it was imperative that all individuals interviewed were evangelical Christians. Grandparents who professed evangelical faith were located by selecting evangelical churches through the Evangelical Free Church of America denomination and gaining access through membership lists. Research was limited to grandparents who were actively involved members of those churches. Christian grandparents, for the purpose of this study, are defined as evangelical Christians either single or married (man or woman) who have at least one grandchild under the age of eighteen years and greater than the age of eighteen months who are part of their extended family through birth or adoption. Non-Christian grandparents were not interviewed for this research, as this provides a different type of data.

Limitations were chosen for the purpose of interviewing grandparents who were active grandparents, not those who were expectant grandparents or grandparents with adult grandchildren. For the sake of maintaining a consistent sample in this particular research, expectant grandparents and grandparents with only adult grandchildren were excluded. For the sake of consistency, it was necessary to adhere to the definition of a grandparent and to limit the research to only grandparents to avoid any variances that arise from various belief systems. Multiple studies exist on grandparent style and roles, but none from the evangelical perspective, which is what this research accomplished.

Research Questions

1. What is the grandparent's role in nurturing the faith of future generations according to biblical analysis?
2. What is the perceived role of grandparents in evangelical contexts toward their grandchildren?
3. What are the practices of grandparents in evangelical contexts toward their grandchildren?
4. What variation in grandparent role is influenced by selected demographics? (age of grandchild, age of grandparent, number of grandchildren, living proximity to grandchild, amount of time spent with grandchildren, divorce, and health of relationship to children)

Terminology

Evangelical. David Bebbington's quadrilateral is a helpful outline when defining the characteristics of evangelicals:

> There are four qualities that have been special marks of Evangelical religion: *conversionism*, the belief that lives need to be changed; *activism*, the expression of the gospel in effort; *biblicism*, a particular regard for the Bible; and what may be called *crucicentrism,* a stress on the sacrifice of Christ on the cross. Together they form a quadrilateral of priorities that is the basis for Evangelicalism.[47]

According to the National Association of Evangelicals (NAE), an evangelical is someone who believes in the good news of Jesus' death and resurrection, follows Jesus, is active in missions and social reform, has a high regard for the Bible as the ultimate authority and obeys it teachings, and stresses the sacrifice of Jesus on the cross as making possible the redemption of humanity. The NAE notes, "Many evangelicals rarely use the term 'evangelical' to describe themselves, focusing simply on the core convictions of the triune God, the Bible, faith, Jesus, salvation, evangelism, and discipleship."[48] Due to these specific doctrinal convictions, this research may not be generalizable to individuals or churches that hold divergent theological beliefs.

Grandparent. For the purpose of this research, "grandparent" is defined as an ancestor who is an evangelical Christian, either single or married (man or woman), who has at least one grandchild under the age of eighteen years and greater than the age of eighteen months who is part of the extended family through birth or adoption.

Intergenerational/multigenerational. Intergenerational relationships, according to Howard Vanderwell, are those "in which people of every age are understood to be equally important."[49] James White defines intergenerational religious education as "two or more different age groups of people in a religious community together learning/growing/living in faith through in-common-experiences, parallel learning, contributive-occasions, and interactive-sharing."[50]

Roles. Grandparenting roles are those that "call for a grandparent's active involvement in a grandchild's life."[51] "The roles grandparents play express both form and substance of grandparenting. . . . These roles satisfy the diverse needs that grandchildren and grandparents have for one another."[52]

Spiritual formation. Spiritual formation is defined as a distinctly Christian process, rooted in God's self-revelation in Jesus Christ through the work of the Spirit rather than the human response to a universal sense of transcendence. This perspective is evident in Paul's words to the church in Colossae: "We proclaim Him, warning and teaching Christ. I labor for this, striving with His strength that works powerfully in me" (Col 1:28-29). James Wilhoit's definition is also helpful to consider: "Spiritual formation (really *trans*formation) is the process, in Paul's language, of 'putting on the Lord Jesus Christ, and not organizing our lives around the satisfaction of our natural desires'" (Rom 13:24). Wilhoit adds, "In that process we 'put off the old man, which is corrupt according to the deceitful lusts, and are renewed in the spirit of our mind; and … put on the new man, which after God is created in righteousness and true holiness'" (Eph 4:22-24).[53]

Procedural Overview

The first phase of the research consisted of a study of biblical content surrounding the role of grandparents toward future generations, explored the historical state of grandparenthood in America from the Industrial Revolution to present day, and included a sociological analysis of the role prescribed to grandparents in American society.

The historical and sociological portions were designed to synthesize existing research into themes that describe society's views of grandparenthood. Biblical findings helped shape interview questions so that contrast and comparison between biblical role and present-day grandparent style could occur. At the end of the first phase of the study interview questions were pilot tested and revised multiple times to ensure the correct data would be gathered.

In order to most effectively establish a sample for the second phase of the study, a combination of purposive and random sampling was utilized. The 2010 United States Census was utilized to locate the five most populated states of older adults. After the states had been identified, a list of all churches registered with the Evangelical Free Church of America in each state was randomly generated.[54]

Beginning with the first five randomly selected churches from each of the five states, a pastor at each church was contacted by email to request inclusion in the study. Twenty-five grandparents were interviewed for this study, distributed between the participating churches. The interviews occurred by phone, consisted of three primary sections, each with four to eight questions, and lasted no more than sixty minutes. Grandparents were asked to limit their answers to grandchildren eighteen years old and younger. The questions were designed to identify the grandparents' perception of their role, identify any variation in role due to life factors (i.e., age of grandchildren, number of grandchildren, proximity to the grandchild, etc.), and gauge any spiritual practices the grandparents are performing on a regular basis. Grandparents were asked a series of questions about their relationship with their grandchildren and role in their grandchildren's life.

Research Assumptions

This study operated under a variety of assumptions.

1. Grandparents involved in this study understand the Bible to be the authoritative base for understanding the role and relationship between grandparent and grandchild.
2. Grandparents that attend evangelical churches identified for this study are evangelicals themselves, confirmed through a membership process by which the grandparent agreed to the church's doctrinal statement.
3. Grandparents will act in a way that accurately reflects their role with their grandchildren.

Notes

1. Rob Rienow, *Visionary Parenting: Capture a God-Sized Vision for Your Family* (Nashville: Randall House, 2009), 17.
2. John Piper, *Rethinking Retirement: Finishing Life for the Glory of Christ* (Wheaton, IL: Crossway, 2009), 5.
3. Ibid., 23-27.
4. Kurt Luscher and Karl Pillemer, "Intergenerational Ambivalence: A New Approach to the Study of Parent-Child Relationships in Later Life," *Journal of Marriage and the Family* 60, no. 2 (1998): 1-32. This article was written from a non-Christian perspective. If non-Christians have observed and are concerned with the ambivalence of the older generation toward younger generations, then how much more concerning should this be for the church?
5. Andrew D. Blechman, *Leisureville: Adventures in a World without Children* (New York: Grove, 2008).
6. Arthur Kornhaber, *Contemporary Grandparenting* (Thousand Oaks, CA: Sage, 1996), 7.
7. Ibid., 11.
8. John Roberto, "Our Future Is Intergenerational," *CEJ* 9, no. 1 (2012): 106.
9. Vern L. Bengtson, "Beyond the Nuclear Family: The Increasing Importance of Multigenerational Bonds," *Journal of Marriage and Family* 63, no. 1 (2001): 1-16.
10. Jeronimo Gonzalez Bernal and Raquel de la Fuente Anuncibay, "Intergenerational Grandparent/Grandchild Relations: The Socioeducational Role of Grandparents," *Educational Gerontology* 34 (2008): 67-88.
11. Bernal and Anuncibay, "Intergenerational Grandparent/Grandchild Relations," 67-88.
12. Bernice L. Neugarten and Karol K. Weinstein, "The Changing American Grandparent," *Journal of Marriage and Family* 26, no. 2 (1964): 199-204.
13. Helen Kivnic, *The Meaning of Grandparenthood* (Ann Arbor, MI: UMI Research Press, 1982).
14. Holly Catterton Allen, "Bringing the Generations Back Together: Introduction to Intergenerationality," *CEJ* 9, no. 1 (2012): 101-4.
15. Kornhaber, *Contemporary Grandparenting*. 3.
16. US Census, "The Older Population: 2010," 3, accessed October 25, 2012, http://www.census.gov/prod/cen2010/briefs/c2010br-09.pdf.
17. Hal Pettigrew, "Perspectives on the Spiritual Development of the 'Aging' Boomers," *CEJ* 5, no. 2 (2008): 305-20.
18. Gary McIntosh, "Trends and Challenges for Ministry among North America's Largest Generation," *CEJ* 5, no. 2 (2008): 294-304.

19. Diana R. Garland, *Family Ministry: A Comprehensive Guide* (Downers Grove, IL: IVP, 1999), 579.

20. James Davies, "A Practical Theology of Aging: Biblical Perspectives for Individuals and the Church," *CEJ* 5, no. 2 (2008): 275-93.

21. Beth E. Brown, "Spiritual Formation in Older Adults," in *The Christian Educator's Handbook on Spiritual Formation*, ed. Kenneth O. Gangel and James C. Wilhoit (Grand Rapids: Baker, 1994), 258.

22. McIntosh, "Trends and Challenges for Ministry," 306.

23. Holly Catterton Allen with Heidi Schultz Oschwald, "The Spiritual Influence of Grandparents," *CEJ* 5, no. 2, (2008): 347.

24. Doreen Maria Mills, "A Pastoral Theological Response to Grandparents Parenting Grandchildren" (Th.M. thesis, Southern Baptist Theological Seminary, 1998), 1.

25. Sharon V. King et al., "The Religious Dimension of the Grandparent Role in Three-Generation African American Households," *Journal of Religion, Spirituality & Aging* 19, no. 1 (2006): 75-96.

26. Allen and Oschwald, "The Spiritual Influence of Grandparents," 347.

27. Mills, "A Pastoral Theological Response," 5.

28. Allen and Oschwald, "The Spiritual Influence of Grandparents," 349.

29. See Neugarten and Weinstein, "The Changing American Grandparent"; Arthur Kornhaber and Kenneth L. Woodward, *Grandparents/Grandchildren: The Vital Connection* (Garden City, NY: Anchor / Doubleday, 1981); Donald C. Reitzes and Elizabeth J. Mutran, "Grandparent Identity, Intergenerational Family Identity, and Well-Being," *The Journals of Gerontology: Psychological and Social Sciences* 59B, no. 4 (2004a; 2004b): 213-19; 9-16.

30. Wesley Ryan Steenberg, "Effective Practices for Training Parents in Family Discipleship: A Mixed Methods Study" (Ph.D. diss., Southern Baptist Theological Seminary, 2011), 3.

31. See Ps 71:17-18; 2 Tim 1:5; Deut 4:9; 6:1-2; Gen 31:55.

32. Roberto, "Our Future Is Intergenerational," 109.

33. Casey Copen and Merril Silverstein, "Transmission of Religious Beliefs across the Generations: Do Grandparents Matter?" *Journal of Comparative Family Studies* 38, no. 4 (2007): 497-510.

34. Blechman, *Leisureville*, 4.

35. Ibid., 4.

36. Ibid., 128.

37. Ibid., 7.

38. Ibid., 8, 13.

39. Ibid., 17.

40. Ibid., 132-35.

41. American Association of Retirement Communities, accessed October 5, 2012, http://www.the-aarc.org.

42. Blechman, *Leisureville*, 26.

43. Ibid., 21-25, 27.

44. "The Retirement City: A New Way of Life for the Old," *Time Magazine*, August 1962, accessed October 5, 2012, www.time.com/time/magazine/article/0,9171,896472,00.html.

45. Blechman, *Leisureville*, 32.

46. Betty Shannon Cloyd, *Parents & Grandparents as Spiritual Guides* (Nashville: Upper Room, 2000). See also Steven Bly and Janet Bly, *The Power of a Godly Grandparent: Leaving a Spiritual Legacy* (Kansas City, MO: Beacon Hill, 2003).

47. David W. Bebbington, *Evangelicalism in Modern Britain: A History from the 1730s to the 1980s* (Florence, KY: Routledge, 1989), 2-3.

48. National Association of Evangelicals, "What Is an Evangelical," accessed October 5, 2012, www.nae.net/church-and-faith-partners/what-is-an-evangelical.

49. Howard Vanderwell, *The Church of All Ages* (Herndon, VA: The Alban Institute, 2008), 11.

50. James White, *Intergenerational Religious Education: Models, Theory, and Prescription for Interage Life and Learning in the Faith Community* (Birmingham, AL: Religious Education, 1988), 18.

51. Kornhaber, *Contemporary Grandparenting*. 90.

52. Ibid., 88.

53. James Wilhoit, *Spiritual Formation as If the Church Mattered* (Grand Rapids: Baker, 2008), 9.

54. The NAE was asked to participate in this study, but declined. The EFCA was chosen because they share a similar doctrinal alignment with the NAE. The EFCA website claims, "We are committed to Jesus Christ, to the gospel and to one another." In addition, the EFCA is committed to teaching biblical truth and has a high view of Scripture. In 1884, several evangelical churches joined together around shared doctrine and values. One of the shared values from the early years of the EFCA was "caring for the elderly." Evangelical Free Church of America, "Who We Are," accessed October 5, 2012, www.efca.org/explore/who-we-are. The EFCA has, at its foundation, understood the value of elderly grandparents, the role of families to care for aging parents, and highlighted these biblical teachings as central to their ministry. As a result of both doctrine and value, the EFCA is a good choice to utilize as a sample population for research related to this dissertation.

CHAPTER 3

Grandparenthood in the Bible

Understanding the Biblical Role of Grandparents

The following section provides an overview of biblical terms and phrases related to grandparenthood as well as highlights biblical themes that inform the role and responsibility grandparents have in the spiritual formation of grandchildren.

Terms and Phrases

The term "grandparent" is a biblical term, but is seldom used in Scripture. As a result of its limited use, some scholars claim grandparents appear on the periphery of Scripture.[1] If a researcher is making this conclusion based on the usage of the term "grandparent" or even the term "old age," such a position may be defendable.[2] For example, the word *grandparent* only occurs two times in the Bible: (1) "And they (locusts) shall fill your houses and the houses of all your servants and of all the Egyptians, as neither your fathers nor your *grandfathers* have seen, from the day they came on the earth to this day" (Exod 10:6).[3] (2) "I am reminded of your sincere faith, a faith that dwelt first in your *grandmother* Lois and your mother Eunice and now, I am sure, dwells in you as well" (2 Tim 1:5).

Despite the limited use of the term "grandparent," the Bible has other ways of referring to grandparents.[4] The word grandfather is taken from two Hebrew words that are equivalent to the phrase "the father of his father." Grandchild is equivalent to "the son of his son."[5] Biblical phrases such as "forefather," "father's father," "God of your fathers," and "children's children," depending on context, may reference grandparenthood.[6] Thus, references to grandparents are common in the Bible.[7]

"I am the God of Your Fathers"

One of God's introductions is to refer to himself as the God of Abraham, Isaac, and Jacob (Acts 3:13; Exod 3:6).[8] For the Israelites, this is comparable to saying "I am the God of your great-great grandfather, great-grandfather, and grandfather."[9] The phrase "God of your fathers" is used twenty-one times in the Bible.[10] Similar phrases, "the God of Abraham," "the God of Isaac," and "the God of Jacob" occur a total of thirty-two times in the Bible.[11] Christopher Wright summarizes the biblical use of the term "the fathers" by stating that it "collectively describes the ancestors of Israel and roots Israel's existence in God's loving election of 'the fathers.'"[12]

There are three theologically significant reasons these phrases are repeated over fifty times in Scripture. (1) These phrases are a reminder of the nature of God as faithful to past generations (Deut 4:37-40; Josh 21:43; 1 Sam 12:7-8).[13] (2) These phrases drew the younger generation's attention to God's everlasting covenant with their forefathers.[14] (3) These phrases call younger generations to walk in obedience to God and warn of the consequences of disobedience.[15] Each time this phrase is read in Scripture, it is identifying God as a multigenerational God who is faithful to ancestors and is worthy of being obeyed and followed by present generations.[16]

"Children's Children"

A second way the Bible speaks of familial grandparenthood is using the phrase "children's children." The Hebrew word "bēn," meaning son, "can be used together with other relationship terms to denote various family relationships: thus, bēn bēn, son's son (Gen 45:10) means 'grandson.'"[17]

The phrase "children's children" is primarily used as a reminder that God's blessings and curses apply to multiple generations and not just individual persons.[18] In Psalm 103:17, God declares he is faithful to those who keep his covenant promises, "but the steadfast love of the Lord is from everlasting to everlasting on those who fear him, and his righteousness to children's children, to those who keep his covenant."[19] In his commentary on Psalms, John Calvin states, "By taking our children's children into his care, he shows how precious to him is our salvation."[20] In contrast, parents who reject the Lord and do not walk in his ways may experience negative consequences for both themselves and their descendants: "There I still contend with you, declares the Lord, and with your children's children I will contend" (Jer 2:9).[21]

Old Age

Old age and grandparenthood are separate but interrelated subjects in Scripture.[22] The author of Proverbs connects old age and grandchildren together when he states that "grandchildren are a crown to the aged" (Prov 17:6). From a biblical perspective, grandparenting encourages grandparents to see one's old days as good days.[23] For centuries, old age has been referred to as *Senectus ipsa morbus est* (old age is itself a disease).[24] Occasionally, a scholar will suggest that the Bible speaks of old age, and therefore grandparenthood, in negative terms due to its use of the phrase "days of sorrow/darkness" and will point to the feebleness and infirmities of those who are old in the narrative of Scripture.[25] However, many scholars agree that "old age is portrayed generally in positive terms, such as 'a crown of glory,' a divine blessing, an honorable life stage, and a wisdom repository."[26] This perspective suggests that grandparenthood, a hallmark of old age, shares these same distinctions.[27] Grandparent, in one word, conveys authority, wisdom, judgment, and status.[28]

Grandparents of contemporary society often lament old age and would benefit from the Bible's perspective of this time of life. The Bible recognizes "the weakness and physical limitations of old age, but in a neutral way, without dwelling on them, and without bitterness."[29] One scholar states that "old age in general is viewed realistically, and old people fare well in the Old Testament."[30] In his book *The Bible Speaks on Aging*, Frank Stagg believes that in Scripture "old age is esteemed."[31] Another scholar notes, "The Proverbs and Psalms compete with one another in heaping praises on the old" (see Prov 16:31; 20:29; 10:27; 4:10; Ps 55:23; 91:16).[32] This same scholar notes, "Old age was habitually qualified as 'good': Abraham 'died in a good old age, an old man and full of years (Gen 25:8).'"[33]

Why was old age good? Old age is a divine blessing, in part, so that grandparents can be a source of godly wisdom for future generations. In addition, the ancients believed achieving old age and having many grandchildren was a sign of God's favor and something to celebrate[34]: "You shall know also that your offspring shall be many, and your descendants as the grass of the earth. You shall come to your grave in ripe old age" (Job 5:25-26).

Grandparents are encouraged to intentionally use their old age to influence grandchildren to love the Lord.[35] The Psalmist informs his readers that "the years of our life are seventy, or even by reason of strength eighty" (v. 90:10).[36] Therefore, "teach us to number our days" (v. 90:12). Grandparents should want to strategically use every minute of life rather than squander any of it.[37] The Psalmist prayed that God would establish the work of his hands (v. 90:17) and that the glories of the Lord would be shown to future generations (v. 90:16).[38] As grandparents enter a new season of life, they must ask themselves, "How am I to live out the remaining years of my life in a way that will glorify God?" Older adults in Christ, including grandparents, are admonished to invest in the younger generations (Titus 2:2-5) and this begins with their family (Pss 78:1-8).

Key Biblical Themes

The Bible speaks of grandparents as important figures in the narrative of Scripture whose role is to pass on faith to future generations. Six themes are considered in this section: heritage of faith, inheritance, the blessing of grandchildren, honoring grandparents, the sin of fathers, and teaching grandchildren.

Heritage of Faith

One word that describes a grandparent's role biblically is the word heritage. Christian scholars Conroy and Fahey believe grandparents are strategically placed to be transmitters of heritage. Conroy and Fahey use the words "crucial" and "key function" to describe the role of grandparents as heritage builders.[39] Joel Ajayi summarizes his research by stating, "An authoritative heritage [is] passed on to the present generation from the ancestors (Deut 32:7; Ps 78; Job 8:12, 15; Prov 4:1-9)."[40]

Grandparents have inherited a faith they are to pass on to their grandchildren (Deut 6:4-9; Ps 71:16-18).[41] This transmission of faith is part of the biblical idea of heritage. Biblically, each member of the family has been given an important, God-ordained role that is not interchangeable with other members of the family. The husband is given the role as the head of the home (Eph 5:23), the wife has the unique role as the man's helpmate (Gen 2:18, 20; Eph 5:22), the child's role is to honor parents through obedience (Exod 20:12; Eph 6:1-3), and the grandparent's role is to be a heritage builder (Pss 78:1-8; 62-63). This is the conviction of Ruth and Elmer Towns:

> What can a grandfather give to his grandchildren when he has nothing left to give? The most important thing that you can give to your grandchildren is not money, possessions, or even the homestead. The most important thing is a *spiritual heritage* to guide their life (italics theirs).[42]

Passing on a heritage, from a biblical perspective, includes communicating key teachings, traditions, and values. According to Ajayi, heritage is passed on when grandparents provide direct instruction to younger generations, through blessings, counsel, guidance, and by righteous living.[43]

The word "heritage" in Scripture refers to a legacy or inheritance and the taking, leaving, becoming, or maintaining of a possession.[44] What is the heritage that grandparents are to pass on to their grandchildren?[45] The one component of heritage that is specific to grandparents is the salvation of grandchildren.[46] Carl Muller believes grandparents play a central and significant role in the salvation of grandchildren.[47] James Meeks notes, "Inheritance language (inheritance, inherit, heir, etc.) is used sixty-five times in the New Testament."[48] According to Meeks, "Over forty times, this terminology refers to the eternal inheritance secured for us by Christ."[49]

The storyline of Scripture reminds grandparents to guard themselves from the assumption that grandchildren will come to salvation in Christ. Many of the Jewish people were guilty of this error.[50] They believed they were participants in God's covenant due to their family heritage as descendants of Abraham (Eph 2:11-18).[51] Grandparents bless grandchildren when they proclaim the gospel and avoid the dangerous assumption that being born into a godly home or being raised in a strong church will lead to the grandchild's salvation.

Inheritance

The Bible suggests that it is a grandparent's role to leave grandchildren with an inheritance. Proverbs 13:22 states, "A good man leaves an inheritance to his children's children."[52] The norm of Scripture is stated in Proverbs 19:14: "House and wealth are inherited from fathers." The Bible speaks of two ways grandparents leave an inheritance: (1) financial, money is transferred to the coming generations; and (2) reputation, a name is passed on and either brings honor or shame.[53]

Whether grandparents have much or little wealth, the greatest inheritance they can give their family is a godly heritage that is passed down from one generation to the next. However, a godly inheritance does not negate a grandparent's responsibility to pass down a financial inheritance; both are the expectation of Scripture.[54]

The biblical concept of inheritance has been lost on many Americans today.[55] Some grandparents spend their financial inheritance on themselves, thinking little about the financial needs of the coming generations.[56] A common bumper sticker confirms the popularity of this line of thinking: "I'm spending my child's inheritance." The pattern of Scripture is to leave one's children and children's children with an inheritance, that being a portion of the grandparent's estate.[57] God modeled inheritance giving by blessing Abraham *and* his descendants with land (Gen 12:7).[58] The important consideration is that the Bible is not silent on this issue, suggesting it is something grandparents should give thought to.

The second way that grandparents provide an inheritance for their grandchildren is by passing on a good name. "A good name," states the author of Ecclesiastes, "is better than precious ointment" (7:1).[59] A good name is valuable.[60] A grandparent's reputation matters as it impacts future generations for good or bad. Ruth and Elmer Towns state,

> When a grandfather can no longer walk down a trail with his grandchildren, nor is he physically able to sit and talk with his grandchildren. When they come for a visit, what can he do? A grandfather can put *his name* upon them, as well as the *name of the Lord*; who will always be with the grandchildren.[61]

The Blessing of Grandchildren

The Bible states that to know one's grandchildren is a blessing. Psalm 128:6 suggests that it is desirable to live long enough to see one's grandchildren: "May you see your children's children!"[62] Biblically, grandparents are held in high esteem, and it is a grandchild that bestows this honor to a grandparent. Proverbs 17:6 states, "Grandchildren are a crown of the aged."[63] Commenting on this passage, Roland Murphy states, "The grandparents are honored in that they have lived a long life and are able to behold their descendants."[64] Numerous examples of this reality exist in Scripture. For example, Jacob felt honored to see his grandchildren. In Job one reads, "After this Job lived 140 years, and saw his sons, and his sons' sons, to the fourth generation" (42:16). In the long list of genealogies found in 1 Chronicles, the large number of grandchildren to Ulam is singled out and spoken of as a blessing: "The sons of Ulam were men who were mighty warriors, bowmen, having many sons and grandsons, 150." According to the Bible, knowing one's grandchildren is desirable and a blessing.

One of the ways God judges the unrighteous is to wipe out their descendants from the earth. "You will destroy their descendants from the earth, and their offspring from among the children of man" (Ps 21:10).[65] King David prayed that wicked and deceitful men would not have grandchildren. "May his posterity be cut off, may his name be blotted out in the second generation!" (Ps 109:13).[66] The Bible implies that God may prohibit some parents from becoming grandparents as a form of judgment for wickedness. For example, Psalm 37:28 promises that children of the wicked shall be cut off. Alternately, the children of the righteous shall be blessed: "Blessed is the man who fears the Lord, who greatly delights in his commandments! His offspring will be mighty in the land; the generation of the upright will be blessed" (Ps 112:1-2).[67]

Honoring Grandparents

Steven Sapp sees the fifth commandment as the "central teaching" on the subject of grandparenthood.[68] Sapp notes that the location of the commandment as the first one addressed to humans governs all interpersonal relationships and functions as the foundation for social morality.[69] The word "honor" means to revere, to hold in awe, to value at a high price.[70] The implication, based on Sapp's assertion, is that grandchildren are to have an attitude of honor, respect, and reverence toward grandparents all the days of their life. Paul Wegner summarizes the reasons honor is to be given to grandparents:

> (a) their belief that God granted long life as a sign of his blessing to people who were righteous and pleasing to him; (b) their belief that persons of greater age acquired knowledge and wisdom from which others could benefit; and (c) if the Israelite culture was largely illiterate, as some have suggested, older people were the main source of oral history and traditions.[71]

Honoring grandparents is demonstrated by positive action on their behalf—meeting their needs, listening to their advice, recognizing their worth, and doing so in all sorts of ways large and small.[72] Grandparents are honored when young people listen to their wisdom.[73] Just as grandparents have a responsibility to invest in a grandchild's spiritual life, grandchildren have the responsibility to honor their grandparents.

The Sin of Fathers Becomes the Sin of Families

A key theme related to grandparents in the Bible is the multigenerational consequence of sin.[74] Second Kings 17:41 makes the point, "So these nations feared the Lord and also served their carved images. Their children did likewise, and their children's children—as their fathers did, so they do to this day." Sin in the life of a grandparent can have a disastrous influence on grandchildren.[75] These passages of Scripture reinforce the need for grandparents to live in obedience to the Lord as a life of sin influences future generations to follow in a similar path.[76]

The Bible provides numerous examples of sin being passed from generation to generation. After the flood, Noah became drunk and lay on the floor of his tent naked. Ham, Noah's son, saw him naked and mocked him to his two brothers.[77] What happens next is surprising. Noah remains silent over Ham, who committed the sin, and curses his grandson Canaan for Ham's sin of mockery (Gen 9:25).[78] Interestingly, these are Noah's only recorded words in Scripture. With his words, Noah inflicts a severe punishment on his grandson. In this instance, the sins of Ham reached to the tenth generation as the entire seed of Canaan was cursed and the fate of the Canaanites was sealed.[79] The Canaanites are listed in Genesis 10:15-19 and are the very nations the Israelites conquered and whose lands they inhabited (Gen 15:18-21; Exod 3:8; 17; Num 13:29; Josh 3:10). The laws provided in Leviticus 18 give some idea of the moral decay of the Canaanite society, their religious practices, and a picture of how they lived. God warned the Israelites to be separate from sinful nations and not to become like the Canaanites (Exod 34:10-17; Deut 7).[80]

Noah, who was cast as a new Adam, and spoken of as one of the godliest men to walk the face of the earth, failed by drinking from the vine, which led to his grandson Canaan's laughter and subsequent curse (Gen 9:20-25). Dempster recognizes that Noah's drunken episode powerfully impacts future descendants in two ways. First, original sin is passed from parent to child to grandchild. Dempster explains, "The fact that Canaan, the 'son' of Ham, is cursed, and not Ham, shows the biblical understanding that the curse registers an impact on the generations."[81] Second, not only is the nature of sin passed on, but also the practice of sin is transmitted through the generations. The first example of generational consequence for sin is seen in the genealogy of Cain. Dempster notes, "This short genealogical notice communicates profound theology. . . . Cain's nonchalant words and his great-great-grandson's boast frame this genealogy and mark its spirit and its descent into a moral and spiritual abyss."[82]

The disastrous effects of sin that governed Cain's descendants makes the warning of Exodus 20:5-6 all the more potent:

> You shall not bow down to them or serve them, for I the Lord your God am a jealous God, visiting the iniquity of the fathers on the children to the third and fourth generation of those who hate me, but showing steadfast love to thousands who love me and keep my commandments.[83]

The choices that grandparents make are not meaningless. They impact families for generations to come.[84]

This truth is also evident in the life of Abraham and throughout the books of 1 and 2 Kings. Abraham lied to Pharaoh and to Abimilech, telling them that Sarah was his sister, not his wife (Gen 20).[85] One of the saddest consequences of Abraham's sin was Isaac's repetition of it years later (Gen 26:7-11) and his grandson Jacob's imitation as well.[86] In fact, Jacob's name means deceiver; this sin became so ingrained in the family that it became part of the family identity. Sin's impact is far-reaching and long-lasting, but it does not have to be permanent.

If grandchildren become aware of ingrained, habitual family sin they can follow the command of Leviticus 26:40 and confess "the iniquity of their fathers,"[87] and the Lord will hear their prayer and forgive them of their family's sin.[88] God works through the confession of his people to break the chains of generational sin.[89] Kittler's research confirms what the Bible teaches:

> It would seem that there is empirical support for the notion that not only does parental religious involvement have a significant effect upon the next generation . . . but so also does grandparental religious involvement have a significant effect upon the next but one generation. It is not only the sins of the grandparent that are visited upon the grandchildren, but also their religious blessing.[90]

Imbedded in God's character is a reminder of his faithfulness to the generations. In Exodus 34:6-7 God states,

> The Lord, a God merciful and gracious, slow to anger, and abounding in steadfast love and faithfulness, keeping steadfast love for thousands [of generations], forgiving iniquity and transgression and sin, but who will by no means clear the guilty, visiting the iniquity of the fathers on the children and the children's children, to the third and fourth generation.[91]

God, in his mercy, provides life and forgiveness through the person and work of Jesus to generation upon generation.

Teaching Grandchildren

According to Keith Kittler and Roy Zuck, Deuteronomy 4:9 and Psalm 78 are texts that speak to the role of grandparents.[92] Kittler summarizes the role of grandparents in Scripture with the following thought:

The importance of the role of grandparents in passing on faith and belief to their grandchildren is well established in Jewish and Christian tradition. Biblical reference is made in Exodus 10:2, Deuteronomy 4:9, and Psalms 78:5-8 to the significance of grandparents in this capacity. In the New Testament, Paul makes reference to the extent to which the faith of grandparents can encourage faith in their grandchildren by showing his confidence in Timothy's faith.[93]

One final theme of grandparenting can be found in Deuteronomy 4:9 where God commands grandparents to follow his laws and teach them to their children's children.[94] Grandparents are instructed to pass faith on to grandchildren and the method of transmission is through teaching. Central to a grandparent's role is verbally communicating the truths of God's Word to grandchildren. Picking up on this theme, Boice suggests Psalm 78 encourages the older generation to teach the younger generation "lessons as to who God is, what he has done, how the people responded to him wrongly in the past, and how they should learn from those past failures today" so that history does not repeat itself and result in unbelief.[95] According to Scripture, one of the central tasks of grandparents is to teach grandchildren the words of God and the works the Lord has done.

God's command to grandparents to teach his commands to grandchildren suggests that Christians are people of the story and they need grandparents to pass on this story.[96] Grandparents fulfill the role of being story-persons as they retell the truths of Scripture as well as being "living stories" and modeling the truths of the Bible in daily living.[97]

Summation

Grandparents have an important role to play in Scripture. Grandparents are entrusted with the task of transferring faith from one generation to the next and passing on a godly heritage to future generations. Throughout the storyline of Scripture, grandparents are seen teaching, worshiping, modeling, and obeying, all with the central purpose of pointing younger generations to the Lord.

A biblical understanding of the place and purpose of grandparents empowers grandparents for continued service in the family and church. The grandparent's role is to leave a godly legacy and build a rich heritage in the Lord. As grandparents transfer faith from one generation to the next, they build their family faith heritage, but ultimately they build God's heritage.[98]

Numerous themes emerge from the biblical study of grandparent-hood. First, according to the Bible, each member of the family has been given an important, God-ordained role that is not interchangeable with other members of the family. Grandparents are given the role of passing a Godly heritage to future generations. Second, the pattern of Scripture is to leave children and grandchildren with an inheritance, that being a portion of the grandparent's estate. Third, the Bible claims that grandchildren are a blessing to grandparents and should be valued by grandparents. Fourth, grandchildren have a biblical responsibility to honor grandparents and care for them in their old age. Fifth, Scripture reinforces the need for grandparents to live in obedience to the Lord as a life of sin influences future generations to follow in a similar sinful path. Alternately, grandparents are to walk in God's ways and devote themselves to seeing their grandchildren do the same. Sixth, the Bible speaks to a spiritual practice that grandparents may employ to accomplish their God-given role. Grandparents are expected to pass on faith to future generations by teaching the truth of Scripture and by telling grandchildren of the work of the Lord.

Notes

1. Joel A. A. Ajayi, *A Biblical Theology of Gerassapience* (New York: Peter Lang, 2010), 111.
2. Scholars identify a range of 100 to 235 occurrences of the of the term זקן in the Old Testament, each use providing a picture of the place and purpose of the elderly in society and family. For more, see Ajayi, *A Biblical Theology of Gerassapience*, 93. Steven Sapp calculates 250 references to old age in the Old Testament alone. Steven Sapp, *Full of Years: Aging and the Elderly in the Bible and Today* (Nashville: Abingdon, 1987), 22.

3. Numerous commentators translate "grandfather" used by the ESV as forefather. Peter Enns, *Exodus*, The NIV Application Commentary (Grand Rapids: Zondervan, 2000), 224. Douglas K. Stuart, *Exodus*, New American Commentary, vol. 2 (Nashville: B & H, 2006), 244.

4. Gordon Harris, who wrote a biblical theology on aging, believes the Bible addresses the subject of old age, and therefore grandparenthood, indirectly using stories, poetry, and character studies. J. Gordon Harris, *Biblical Perspectives on Aging: God and the Elderly* (New York: Haworth, 2008), 12.

5. Harlan J. Wechsler, "Judaic Perspectives on Grandparenthood," in *Grandparenthood*, ed. Vern L. Bengtson and Joan F. Robertson (Beverly Hills: Sage, 1985), 187.

6. Edward W. Goodrick and John R. Kohlenberger III, *Zondervan NIV Exhaustive Concordance* (Grand Rapids: Zondervan, 1999), 197; 386-87; 413-14; 436.

7. J. W. Drane, "Family," in *New Dictionary of Biblical Theology: Exploring the Unity & Diversity of Scripture*, ed. T. Desmond Alexander et al. (Downers Grove, IL: InterVarsity, 2000), 494.

8. In Exod 3:6, when God was speaking to Moses at the burning bush, he chose to reveal himself as "the God of your father, the God of Abraham, the God of Isaac, and the God of Jacob." Commentator John Durham understands this passage to mean that "what Moses is told must therefore be understood as a means of connecting the speaking deity with the faith of Moses' family in Egypt" a "conscious attempt to identify Yahweh and the God of the fathers as one and the same." John Durham, *Exodus*, Word Biblical Commentary, vol. 3 (Nashville: Thomas Nelson, 1987), 31. Other examples include when Elijah prayed, "O Lord, God of Abraham, Isaac and Israel, let it be known this day that you are God in Israel" (1 Kgs 18:36), and when King David prayed, "O Lord, the God of Abraham, Isaac, and Israel, our fathers, keep forever such purposes and thoughts in the hearts of your people, and direct their hearts toward you" (2 Chr 29:18).

9. When read, this phrase references God's covenant with Israel. God is a multigenerational God, but he is much more than that; he is a covenant-keeping God throughout the generations. Thus, Moses can appeal to God's promised covenant when Israel made a golden calf and the Lord's anger burned against the people. Durham notes that Moses' appeal to God's promise to the fathers, to whom Yahweh had bound himself by oath, moved God to pity for Israel tempering his anger. Durham, *Exodus*, 429. See also Stuart, *Exodus*, 671-72 for helpful explanation of Exodus 32:13 and a connection between God's covenant promise and God's inheritance of a people.

10. Sapp, *Full of Years*, 21. Examples in Scripture include when Jehoshaphat calls out for deliverance from his enemies by saying, "O Lord, God of our fathers, deliver us" (2 Chr 20:6); Elijah passes judgment on King Jehoram by saying, "Thus says the Lord, the God of David your father," for not walking obediently before the Lord you shall get a disease and die (2 Chr 21:12); Ezra praises God for moving in King Artaxerxes' heart to commission him to teach the people the law of the Lord: "Blessed be the Lord, the God of our fathers" (Ezra 7:27); the Psalmist calls people to praise God for his faithfulness to his covenant people despite being put to the test repeatedly by the fathers of Israel (Ps 95:9); Jeremiah asks, "What wrong did your fathers find in me that they went far from me?" (Jer 2:4); Daniel prays to "the God of my fathers" (Dan 2:23); Jesus, in discussion with the Sadducees, refers to God as "the God of Abraham, and the God of Isaac, and the God of Jacob" (Matt 22:32); and the apostles told the council of Sadducees that "the God of our fathers raised Jesus" (Acts 5:30).

11. Ibid., 21.

12. Christopher J. H. Wright, "The Fathers," in *New International Dictionary of Theology and Exegesis*, ed. Willem A. VanGemeren (Grand Rapids: Zondervan, 1997), 1:220.

13. Raymond Brown, *The Message of Deuteronomy*, The Bible Speaks Today (Downers Grove, IL: InterVarsity, 1993), 72. Phrases such as "When the Lord brings you into the land of the Canaanites, as he swore to you, and your fathers," reminded the Israelites that God kept his promises and that they were not the first generation to be in covenant with the Lord (Exod 13:11; Deut 1:11; 12:1). Rob Rienow encourages parents to "imagine Isaac speaking to Jacob and saying, 'Let me tell you about the God of your grandfather Abraham'; utilizing the faith of a grandparent to teach a grandchild who God is and what God has done." Rob Rienow, *Visionary Parenting: Capture a God-Sized Vision for Your Family* (Nashville: Randall House, 2009), 21.

14. John Calvin, *Genesis*, The Crossway Classic Commentaries (Wheaton, IL: Crossway, 2001), 232.

15. The pattern of Scripture is to remind young people of the faith of those who have gone before; this is what brought about revival at the time of Hezekiah (2 Chr 29:5-6). The Bible also warns the younger generation not to repeat the sins of previous generations: "O people of Israel, return to the Lord, the God of Abraham, Isaac, and Israel. . . . Do not be like your fathers and your brothers, who were faithless to the Lord God of their fathers" (2 Chr 29:6-7). If the people of Israel "abandoned the Lord, the God of their fathers" and worshiped other gods, then God promised to bring disaster on his people (2 Chr 7:22; 24:18; 24; 27:9).

16. Stuart notes, "The fact that God identified himself to Moses [in Exod 3:6] through the expression 'the God of your father' is part of the evidence that Yahweh was a name known to the patriarchs and not newly revealed at this time. But the common view remains that this is the point of the invention or introduction of the name Yahweh into Israelite religion." Stuart, *Exodus*, 115.

17. Chrys S. Caragounis, "*bēn*," in *New International Dictionary of Theology and Exegesis*, 1:672.

18. Family, in the Old Testament, was God's vehicle to build his heritage and bless the nations (Ezek 37:24-28). Under the old covenant, God's promise was not to a person, but to a people. God promised to give the nation of Israel land, and that "they and their children and their children's children shall dwell there forever" (Ezek 37:25). God wanted to dwell in their midst so the nations would know it was the Lord God who saved and sanctified the nation of Israel (Ezek 37:27-28; 39:21-23). Ultimately God made a covenant with the forefathers of Israel and promised to multiply them (See Ezek 37:24-28) so the nations would know God. One of the Old Testament motivations to "be fruitful and multiply" is rooted in God's desire to bless the nations. The phrase "children's children" reminds one of God's blessings first to individual families, then to tribes, a nation, and ultimately the world. God blesses families for the purpose of blessing the world so that all people will see the goodness and the greatness of God (Gen 18:18-19).

19. In this passage "David is rousing himself to remember God's benefits, and he does not want to do it superficially. He wants to do it with all his heart, with all his soul, and with all his strength." God is merciful and gracious to many generations and is worthy of wholehearted praise. James Montgomery Boice, *Psalms* (Grand Rapids: Baker, 1993), 2:833.

20. John Calvin, *Commentary on the Psalms* (Carlisle, PA: The Banner of Truth Trust, 2009), 476.

21. Also see Ezek 37:25.

22. What was considered old age according to the Bible? Georges Minois asserts, "Old age began at 60. . . . Any death before the age of 60 was considered premature." Minois claims that in Scripture "people died very old and happy." Georges Minois, *History of Old Age* (Chicago: University of Chicago Press, 1989), 33; 41. In the narrative of Scripture it is not uncommon to find individuals who live a long life. For more see vanThanh Nguyen, "Biblical Perspectives on Caring for the Aged and the Sick," *New Theology Review* 23, no. 4 (2010): 6. In Scripture, there is some indication that a person was considered elderly at the age of 60 (see 1 Tim 5:9). Ajayi suggests that old "ranges in biblical traditions from 60 years to 120 years." Ajayi, *A Biblical Theology of Gerassapience*, 7. In Lev 27:3 there is a distinction made between those who are 20 to 60 years old and those who are over 61 years old indirectly giving weight to the notion that old age occurs at 60. Lev 27:1-8 covers the entire lifespan of humans separating people into three categories: (1) childhood, birth to 20 years old; (2) adulthood, 21 to 60 years old; and (3) the elderly years, 61 years old and older. Supporting this perspective is the life of King Hezekiah, who was told at the age of thirty-nine years old that he would die: "In the noontide of my days I must depart" (Isa 38:10). Hezekiah's use of the word "noontide" does not imply old age, but the middle of life.

23. A handful of individuals have attempted to write biblical theologies on aging or the elderly. Stephen Sapp's *Full of Years* offers one of the most comprehensive chapters on what the Old Testament says about aging. Noting that there is more material than he can cover, Sapp neglects to deal with key individuals and themes. Sapp writes about the New Testament with skepticism, thus limiting the overall value of his work. Gordon Harris wrote a book on the biblical theology of aging titled *Biblical Perspectives on Aging*, which scholars refer to often, some criticizing and others commending. Joel Ajayi has written the most recent biblical theology on aging which he titled *A*

Biblical Theology of Gerassapience. Ajayi emphasizes the connection between old age and wisdom and traces this theme throughout Scripture.

24. Trevor H. Howell, "King Solomon's Portrait of Old Age," *Age and Aging* 16, no. 5 (1987): 331-33.

25. Sheldon Isenberg, "Aging in Judaism: 'Crown of Glory' and 'Days of Sorrow,'" in *Handbook of the Humanities and Aging,* ed. Thomas R. Cole, David D. van Tassel, and Robert Kastenbaum (New York: Springer, 1992), 161. See also Eccl 12:1-7.

26. Ibid.

27. The Bible uses the same language to describe both old age and grandparenthood. See Prov 16:31 and 17:6.

28. Wechsler, "Judaic Perspectives on Grandparenthood," 188.

29. Minois, *History of Old Age,* 31.

30. Don C. Charles, "Literary Old Age: A Browse through History," *Educational Gerontology* 2, no. 3 (1977): 240.

31. Frank Stagg, *The Bible Speaks on Aging* (Nashville: Broadman, 1981), 181.

32. Minois, *History of Old Age,* 29.

33. Ibid., 30. The same could be said of Isaac (Gen 35:29) and Gideon (Jdg 8:32).

34. Alistair I. Wilson and James A. Grant, *The God of Covenant: Biblical, Theological, and Contemporary Perspectives* (Downers Grove, IL: InterVarsity, 2005), 277. Living to old age may be a reward from God for living a life of obedience to his commands: "My son, do not forget my teaching, but let your heart keep my commandments, for the length of days and years of life and peace they will add to you" (Prov 3:1; see also Prov 4:10). W. R. F. Browning, "Old Age," in *Oxford Dictionary of the Bible* (New York: Oxford University Press, 2009), 271. Proverbs repeats this same idea, "Gray hair is a crown of glory; it is gained in a righteous life" (Prov 16:31). The opposite is also true: early death is often depicted in Scriptures as judgment from the Lord for rebellion. For example, God punished Eli's household for the wickedness of Eli's sons and said, "There will not be an old man in your house" (2 Sam 2:31). Eli was judged for honoring his family over the Lord, something grandparents should pay attention to and learn from.

35. Holly Catterton Allen with Heidi Schultz Oschwald, "The Spiritual Influence of Grandparents," *Christian Education Journal* 5, no. 2 (2008): 350.

36. The Bible records the ages of many individuals. Moses died at the age of 120 (Deut 34:7); his brother Aaron died at 123 years old (Num 33:39). Joshua died at 110 (Josh 24:29) while Eli died at 98 years old (1 Sam 4:15-18). Barzillai, who was hospitable to David and his men, died past the age of 80 and David died at 70 (2 Sam 5:4). Jehoida the priest died at 130 years old (2 Chr 24:15) and Job died when he was 140 years old (Job 42:16). This list of individuals is long and could include Caleb, Zechariah, Anna, John, Paul, and many more.

37. Life is short and the grandparent is to remember this reality (see Pss 144:4 and 39:4-7). Job speaks regularly of the brevity of life and God's sovereignty over it: "Since his days are determined, and the number of his months is with you, and you have appointed his limits that he cannot pass" (Job 14:5). The Psalmist says, "O Lord, make me know my end and what is the measure of my days; let me know how fleeting I am!" (Ps 39:4).

38. Steven Sapp states that in the Old Testament, old age was not something to dread as an intrusion into God's intended purpose for human existence, rather it was something one accepted, if not welcomed as a sign of God's favor and reward for righteousness. Sapp, *Full of Years,* 65-67. God designed the elderly years to be an enjoyable season of life. Ecclesiastes reminds the elderly, "If a person lives many years, let him rejoice in them all" (Eccl 11:8). The Bible never speaks of aging as a problem to avoid, but a blessing to embrace. Physical aging is part of God's plan for humanity. The Psalmist suggests that long life is to be viewed as a gift from God (Ps 91:16). The Bible states that gray hair is a "crown of glory" (Prov 16:31).

39. Donald B. Conroy and Charles J. Fahey, "Christian Perspectives on the Role of Grandparents," in *Grandparenthood,* 196.

40. Ajayi, *A Biblical Theology of Gerassapience,* 211.

41. Ajayi refers to this as the social-anthropological role of the elderly and believes that a primary function of old age is to see faith "inheritable" and "transmissible" between generations through the use of traditions. Ibid., 111.

42. Ruth Towns and Elmer Towns, "Grandparents in the Bible: What They Can Teach Us about Influencing Children," 10, emphasis original, accessed February 11, 2014, http://elmertowns.com/wp-content/uploads/2014/01/GrandparentsoftheBible.pdf.

43. Ajayi, *A Biblical Theology of Gerassapience,* 211.

44. Ludwig Koehler and Walter Baumgartner, eds., *The Hebrew and Aramaic Lexicon of the Old Testament* (Boston: Brill, 2001), 1:686. Also see Gary Baldwin, "Heritage," in *Holman Illustrated Bible Dictionary,* ed. Charles W. Draper, Chad Brand, and Archie England (Nashville: Holman Bible, 2003), 752.

45. The concept of inheritance expresses a fundamental relationship between God and his people and reveals God's desire to give his people a secure home. J. Eichler, "Inheritance," in *New International Dictionary of New Testament Theology,* ed. Colin Brown (Grand Rapids: Zondervan, 1976), 2:295.

46. James Hester suggests an inheritance is something that (1) is given, normally by testament, (2) continues to remain in possession, inalienable property, (3) is a family possession, a patrimony, and (4) may be conveyed by adoption to persons originally outside the family. James D. Hester, *Paul's Concept of Inheritance: A Contribution to the Understanding of Heilsgeschichte* (Edinburgh: Oliver and Boyd, 1968), vii. All four of these elements are present when Scripture speaks of the inheritance as God's heir through salvation; especially the fourth point.

47. Carl Muller, *Unconverted Sons and Daughters: Hope for Hurting Parents* (Leominster, UK: Day One, 2012), 57.

48. Meeks believes the most prominent use of inheritance in the Old Testament was in reference to the land, which was both God's gift and God's inheritance to his people. To see a detailed breakdown of word use for inheritance in the Old Testament, see James A. Meeks, "The Riches of His Inheritance," *Presbyterian* 28, no. 1 (2008): 37.

49. Ibid., 35.

50. Werner Foerster, "Inheritance," in *Theological Dictionary of the New Testament,* ed. Gerhard Kittel and Gerhard Friedrich (Grand Rapids: William B. Eerdmans, 1964), 3:784.

51. Inheritance means "to receive something of considerable value which has not been earned." Johannes P. Louw and Eugene A. Nida, eds., *Greek-English Lexicon of the New Testament Based on Semantic Domains* (New York: United Bible Societies, 1989), s.v. "ηηρονομέω" (section 57:131).

52. Bruce Waltke argues that Prov 13:22 gives grandparents a responsibility to pass anything of value on to future generations: "The person who functions according to that for which he was created gives *[wealth] as an inheritance (yanhii; see 3:21) to his grandchildren* (lit. 'Sons of sons'), signifying that the family inheritance is enduring from generation to generation. *Hayil,* glossed *wealth,* has the essential meaning of 'strength' or 'power' here and functions as a metonymy for any and all valuable property." Bruce K. Waltke, *The Book of Proverbs: Chapters 1-15,* NICOT (Grand Rapids: William B. Eerdmans, 2004), 572, emphasis original.

53. Koehler and Baumgartner, *The Hebrew and Aramaic Lexicon,* 1:686.

54. J. Herrmann, "Inheritance," in *Theological Dictionary of the New Testament,* 3:775.

55. Roland Murphy understands Prov 13:22 to create a contrast between the good and evil person and claims that the "good person . . . will leave a goodly inheritance for his progeny." Roland E. Murphy, *Proverbs,* Word Biblical Commentary, vol. 22 (Nashville: Thomas Nelson, 1998), 98. This responsibility is lost on many Americans today.

56. The Hebrew word for "stored up" in Prov 13:22 (*sāpan*) "entails that the sinner stored his wealth up for some specific purpose. . . . He intended his wealth to serve his greed." Waltke, *The Book of Proverbs,* 572.

57. According to Roland Murphy, "an heir could count on receiving an inheritance," it was "almost automatic, specified by practice or law." Murphy, *Proverbs,* 144.

58. See Wenham for an overview of differing interpretations of "to your descendants I will give this land." Gordon Wenham, *Genesis 1-15,* Word Biblical Commentary, vol. 1 (Nashville: Thomas Nelson, 1987), 279-80.

59. According to commentator J. Stafford Wright, a goal for one's family inheritance is to "preserve your good name until the day of your death." J. Stafford Wright, *Ecclesiastes,* in vol. 5 of *The Expositor's Bible Commentary,* ed. Frank Gaebelein (Grand Rapids: Zondervan, 1991), 1174.

60. Israelites were known by their family name and identified by their "fathers' houses" (Num 1:4; 18; Josh 21:1).

61. Towns and Towns, "Grandparents in the Bible," 9, emphasis original.

62. Commentator Hans‑Joachim Kraus says that a large family, including grandchildren, is a special blessing from God. In addition, Kraus notes that grandchildren are a blessing because they extend a person's limited physical existence through one's children's children. Hans‑Joachim Kraus, *Psalms 60-150*, A Continental Commentary (Minneapolis: Fortress, 1993), 459.

63. Tremper Longman III interprets "crown" to mean reward: "That the elderly have grandchildren at all is testimony to their long lives and their fertility and thus the rewards ("crown") of godliness. Tremper Longman III, *Proverbs*, The Baker Commentary on the Old Testament Wisdom and Psalms (Grand Rapids: Baker, 2006), 344.

64. Murphy, *Proverbs*, 129.

65. Scholars suggest this is a difficult text to interpret. Due to the hard truth of this passage, one scholar believes the passage has been corrupted over time and, as a result, he offers different translations which soften the meaning of the passage. See Francis J. Morrow, Jr., "Psalm 21:10: An Example of Haplography," *Vetus Testamentum* 18, no. 4 (1968): 558-59. Some commentators completely avoid dealing with the passage. For example, see James Montgomery Boice, *Psalms* (Grand Rapids: Baker, 1994), 1:188-89. VanGemeren understands this passage to apply the curses of the covenant to the enemies of the Lord through God's anointed king. Willem A. VanGemeren, *Psalms*, in vol. 5 of *The Expositor's Bible Commentary*, ed. Frank E. Gaebelein (Grand Rapids: Zondervan, 1991), 196.

66. Kraus asks why this curse should come upon a person and his descendants. He answers his own question by stating that the person's guilt is remembered, unforgiven, and imputed. If Kraus is correct, it may also be argued that forgiveness through Christ removes the curse referred to in this Psalm. Kraus, *Psalms 60-150*, 340.

67. John Calvin cautions that parents should not dictate to God how he should bless their progeny, but can hold to the promise of this passage that as the faithful raise their children in the fear of the Lord, God blesses them. Calvin, *Genesis*, 521. Kraus argues that this promise applies to individuals as well as to groups of people. Kraus has noted that God's rewards are real, heaped on the godly in great quantities, and one of those rewards is the quantity and quality of descendants. Kraus, *Psalms 50-160*, 363-64.

68. Sapp, *Full of Years*, 60.

69. Ibid., 82.

70. Koehler and Baumgartner, *The Hebrew and Aramaic Lexicon*, 455.

71. Paul D. Wegner, "Old Age," in *New International Dictionary of Theology and Exegesis*, ed. Willem A. VanGemeren (Grand Rapids: Zondervan, 1997), 1:1136.

72. Stuart, *Exodus*, 461.

73. Browning, "Old Age," 271.

74. For an overview of the phrase "sin of fathers," see Edwin C. Hostetter, "Fruitful," in *New International Dictionary of Theology and Exegesis*, 3:678-79.

75. For more on the nature of sin, its effects on the community, and its consequences, as well as key passages and terms in the Old and New Testament, see Mark E. Biddle, *Missing the Mark: Sin and Its Consequences in Biblical Theology* (Nashville: Abingdon, 2005). One study of over 1.2 million worshippers in over 12,000 congregations in the United Kingdom found a direct correlation between the faith of grandparents and the faith of grandchildren. Keith Kittler, "Who Says Grandparents Matter?" *Journal of Beliefs and Values* 29, no. 1 (2008): 51-60. Science confirms what the Bible claims: as the father and grandfather go, so often do the child and grandchild. A recent study on brain development found that drug use profoundly affects the DNA structure that is passed from generation to generation, making future generations more prone to addiction. Michael D. Scofield and Peter W. Kalivas, "Forgiving the Sins of the Fathers," *Nature Neuroscience* 16, no. 1 (2013): 4-5.

76. Wright summarizes, "The statement that God 'punishes the children for the sin of the fathers to the third and fourth generation' (Exod 20:5; Deut 5:9) must be understood in the context of

solidarity of extended families (of three or four generations living together), in which the sin (especially idolatry) of one generation would affect the others detrimentally; it is not a principle of human judicial action (that is excluded by Deut 24:16). It is more than outweighed by the following 'thousands' of generations God desires to bless for obedience (cf. Deut 7:9) and his definitive forgiving nature (Exod 34:6-7; Num 14:18). Nevertheless, the accumulated sin of generations could be seen as finally justifying God's judgment (2 Kgs 17:14;21:11-15; 22:13), but prophets had to resist the tendency of the generation of the exile to exonerate themselves by laying all the blame on their fathers (Isa 65:7; Jer 31:29-30; Lam 5:7; Ezek 18). The proper response should be repentance and confession that identifies with the sins of the fathers (Lev 26:40; Neh 9:32-34; Ps 106:6; Jer 3:25; Dan 9:8, 16). Wright, "The Fathers," 1:221.

77. Gordon Harris believes Ham committed the sin of disrespect and did not honor his father as God desires. Harris, *Biblical Perspectives on Aging*, 19.

78. Wenham presents three views why Noah cursed Canaan instead of Ham. First, God had recently pronounced his blessing on Noah and his sons, so that Noah could not unsay that promise. Second, there may be a mirroring punishment: here Noah's youngest son, Ham, sinned against him; therefore it was appropriate that Ham's youngest son, Canaan, should be punished for his father's wickedness. Third, the view Wenham favors, the sons of Noah embody and personify the character of their descendants. Wenham, *Genesis 1-15*, 201.

79. Sailhamer suggests this passage creates and contrasts two categories of people; those who are like Adam and Eve and did not look on man's nakedness, but covered it with animal skins, and those who expose their nakedness. John H. Sailhamer, *Genesis*, in vol. 2 of *The Expositor's Bible Commentary*, ed. Frank E. Gaebelein (Grand Rapids: Zondervan, 1990), 96.

80. Moshe Weinfeld notes that God's command not to marry from other nations was given so that Israel would not worship false idols. For more about the nations God commanded the people not to inter-marry with, see Moshe Weinfeld, *Deuteronomy 1-11*, The Anchor Yale Bible Commentary (New Haven, CT: Yale University Press, 1991), 362-66.

81. Stephen G. Dempster, *Dominion and Dynasty: A Theology of the Hebrew Bible*, ed. D. A. Carson (Downers Grove, IL: InterVarsity, 2003), 74.

82. Ibid., 70-71.

83. Durham believes this is covenantal language. He states that those who "hold him [God] in contempt: upon them in result must come a deserved judgment, across four generations . . . but even more, the insight that indifference to commitment is contagious, in a family or in a society." Durham, *Exodus*, 287.

84. R. Albert Mohler, Jr., provides a helpful statement about the phrase "sins of the father": "Some Christians turn these statements into nonsensical and sensationalistic warnings about 'generational curses' that must be removed by some kind of special prayer or ministry. The reality of the biblical warning is clear enough. We are warned that the consequences of our sins are not limited to ourselves or even to our own generation." R. Albert Mohler, Jr., "The Sins of the Father," accessed June 25, 2014, http://www.albertmohler.com/2010/12/14/the-sins-of-the-father/.

85. Westermann sees nothing wrong with Abraham's reference to Sarah as his sister and reasons away this deceptive phrase as simply the introduction to a narrative of Scripture. Claus Westermann, *Genesis 12-36*, A Continental Commentary (Minneapolis: Fortress, 1995), 320.

86. In contrast to Westermann's view, Sailhamer states, "Such similarities can hardly be coincidental. The writer wants to portray to the reader that the lives of the two patriarchs did in fact run a similar course." Sailhamer, *Genesis*, 187.

87. Commenting on this passage, R. Laird Harris states, "Confession is essential if we would be rid of sin and right with God." R. Laird Harris, *Leviticus*, in vol. 2 of *The Expositor's Bible Commentary*, ed. Frank E. Gaebelein (Grand Rapids: Zondervan, 1990), 648.

88. According to the Bible, families should take three steps to deal with sin: acknowledge sin, confess it, and obey God. First, it is important to acknowledge the presence of sin in one's family. "Both we and our fathers have sinned; we have committed iniquity; we have done wickedness. Our fathers, when they were in Egypt, did not consider your wondrous works; they did not remember the

abundance of your steadfast love" (Ps 106:6-7). Second, when sin is found, it should be confessed. "We acknowledge our wickedness, O Lord, and the iniquity of our fathers, for we have sinned against you" (Jer 14:20; 7:25-26; Acts 7:51). Third, sin is to be identified so that future generations do not follow in the same rebellious footsteps of their ancestors. God sent prophets to let the Israelites "know the abominations of their fathers" so that they would not "walk in the statues of your fathers, nor keep their rules, nor defile yourselves with their idols" and would "know that I am the Lord" (Ezek 20:4; 18; 38).

89. Sexual sins are one of the common generational sins referenced in Scripture. In Lev 18:6 God states, "None of you shall approach any one of his close relatives to uncover nakedness." Specifically related to grandparenting God says, "You shall not uncover the nakedness of your son's daughter or of your daughter's daughter, for their nakedness is your own nakedness" (Lev 18:10). God refers to any sexual acts between grandparent and grandchild as "depravity" (Lev 18:17). It is noteworthy that God sets forth household expectations for children, parents, and grandparents, as well as aunts, uncles, stepsiblings, and stepparents.

90. Kittler, "Who Says Grandparents Matter?," 52.

91. Durham suggests this statement about God was produced by the circle of Israel's wise men, refined over time, and used for confessional purposes regarding the nature of God. Durham, *Exodus*, 454.

92. Kittler, "Who Says Grandparents Matter?," 52-53. Roy B. Zuck, *Precious in His Sight: Childhood & Children in the Bible* (Grand Rapids: Baker, 1996), 103; 131-32.

93. Kittler, "Who Says Grandparents Matter?," 52-53.

94. Grammatically and conceptually, the primary command of Deut 4:9-14 is an exhortation to pass down to children and grandchildren that which the oldest generation had seen and knew.

95. Boice also argues Ps 78 echoes Deut 6:6-9. Boice, *Psalms*, 2:645-46.

96. Conroy and Fahey, "Christian Perspectives," 196.

97. Ibid., 196.

98. The Lois Legacy of 2 Tim 1:3-7 is an example to which grandparents can aspire. Lois, the grandmother of Timothy, blessed her grandson with a rich heritage of faith.

PART 3:

CULTURE'S MESSAGES

CHAPTER 4

A Brief History of Grandparenthood in America

Learning from the Multigenerational Mistakes of the Past

Historically, families have operated in a multigenerational manner with grandparents as an essential part of the family.[1] This began to change in the early twentieth century as the narrative of American culture began to encourage a nuclear family structure rather than an extended family mindset.[2] Brian Gratton and Carole Haber suggest that three distinct phases mark the history of American Grandparents: authority figures, burdens, and companions.[3]

Historians make two key arguments as to why the elderly had greater respect and a more important role in preindustrial America: scarcity value and educational role. Elderly people formed a small percentage of the total population of any preindustrial society. Shorter life spans made old age more rare than it is today, and their scarcity compared to contemporary levels increased their value to society. The educational role of the elderly served to orient attitudes toward, and treatment of, grandparents. Preindustrial societies were largely illiterate, and learning depended on word of mouth. The elderly served as society's mentors with an important role of information control.[4] In addition, experience was a valuable attribute for most endeavors and was one value that elders possessed in greater abundance than youthful contemporaries.[5]

The picture of grandparents as an important part of the home began to slowly change as the elderly began to lose authority in the family. With the advance of time the number of elderly people increased and their value as educators decreased. "With modern literacy, learning is stored in books—not old minds—and so the elderly automatically lose status and function."[6] With the advance of medicine, life spans began to increase. Living to old age, which was once rare, was becoming more common.

The American perspective toward elderly parents morphed over a relatively short period of time. One document is particularly helpful as it provides a glimpse into a tectonic shift that occurred nearly a century ago. The article, "Age Old Intestate," was written by an anonymous author in 1931 and describes the changing mindset that adult children had toward their elderly parents.

Throughout history, as parents aged, they went to live in a child's home. The anonymous author suggests this tradition was not simply an American creation, but "an ancient custom of taking the old into the homes of the young."[7] The author's experience suggests tri-generational living was the norm: "When I was a child I took it for granted that a grandmother or grandfather should live in the house of nearly every one of my playmates."[8] In previous generations, the only means of care for the elderly was to go into the homes of their children:

> It has always been taken for granted that when men or women grow old and become lonely or helpless or sick, they should, of course, go to live with sons and daughters. . . . This assumption implies, moreover, that it is necessarily the duty of the young to make home life possible for the old.[9]

By the 1930s, this mindset was beginning to change and the elderly were viewed as a burden to separate from rather than a blessing to incorporate into the family. According to the author, life was great when her parents were independent and isolated from her family, but that changed once her mother moved in. The author portrays elderly parents as a disruption to life and the cause of dysfunction in the family:

> Before then my household of four lived in harmony. My husband and I had found our home restful. We had enjoyed a bit of leisure.... There was nothing present that menaced the foundations of our happiness or the children's welfare.... Now harmony is gone. Rest has vanished. My husband and I have no longer any time together unless we leave the house. We have no leisure. We have no time for children.... We have had to shut our door to hospitality.[10]

The same author boldly declares that she wants little to do with her children and grandchildren as she ages: "We desire to live our lives physically and personally independent of our children."[11] Such a mindset was becoming prevalent in American society.

Family relationships have changed over the past century; there are new expectations regarding how the generations are to interact, when, and in what ways. The industrial revolution altered family structure with the primary function shifting from social-institutional to emotional-supportive. The modern family is nuclear, not extended. A new sense of individualism and the desire for personal privacy has weakened ties between the generations. The decline of the patriarchal idea and a growing desire for economic independence displaced the elderly from a central place in the family and helped fuel age-segregation and a subsidiary role for grandparents.

Social security provided the means for independent living for the elderly. Separate residence for the generations become both desirable and possible in the twenty-first century. One of the clearest indications of the new way of life for the elderly is reflected in living situation. Steven Ruggles suggests that in the 1850s, more than 60 percent of old people shared a home with their children; today less than 15 percent do.[12] Today, grandparents desire a relationship that is "one of 'closeness at a distance,' of basically independent existence."[13] The desire for intimate independence shapes the older generation's contact with younger generations.

Such views fit the newly predominant cultural view of grandparents as independent individuals whose most important responsibility was to maintain their autonomy. Stressing the advantages of retirement, experts warned their readers of the need to be financially secure. No aged person, they argued, should depend on relatives for support.[14]

When the generations successfully achieved independence from one another, there was nothing to anchor them together, and the elderly began to search for a purpose for their remaining years of life. As society fragments, seniors are encouraged to band together and take care of themselves because nobody else will.[15] With no need to work, and limited involvement with family, the place the elderly turned their attention was to themselves. Independence from the generations led to indulgence for themselves. As a result, older adults started viewing autonomy and leisure as the goals of their "golden years."

Because the new role of grandparents was not clearly defined, it came to be viewed as a frill; a role not essential to the functioning of the family or the growth and development of children. Grandparents themselves feared meddling in their children's and grandchildren's lives. So while the relationship, when it existed, could be very positive, its limited and tenuous nature removed grandparents from the central hub of family life and placed them on the periphery with a minimal role.

Grandparents became companions to their grandchildren as independence meant they had no authoritative position or important economic role in the family.[16] Experts counseled grandparents to "strive for love and friendship rather than demand respect and obedience. Grandparents coddled and cuddled rather than disciplined; they listened affectionately rather than spoke authoritatively."[17]

American society rejected the historical role of grandparent as authority and replaced this role with a new role: companionship. Grandparents responded by altering their priorities based on the role society provided. Essentially, grandparents were told they were not wanted or needed in the home for any significant purpose. Society placed grandparents out to pasture and told them they had no role of substance in the home, and were free to pursue other interests. With no significant role in the home and limited financial need to work, grandparents shifted their attention to the only place left: themselves. In general, the past century is the sad tale of grandparents shifting their values from investing in future generations to indulging themselves.

The historical role grandparents had in the home has not disappeared; it has been replaced. "In the absence of grandparents, these functions have been taken over by surrogates which have no personal, lasting, or emotional commitment to children."[18] Surrogates include teachers, peers, psychologists, media, pastors, and celebrities. Sunday dinner at grandmother's house has been replaced by Sunday dinner at a restaurant. Gathering around the fireplace to hear stories of the past has been replaced by gathering around the television to watch a fictional story created by a stranger. Dropping a grandchild off at grandfather's house has been replaced by dropping the grandchild off at a daycare center. Grandparents who abdicate their role have created a void that has been filled by others.

Notes

1. For more information on the history of grandparenthood in America, see Josh Mulvihill, "A New Way of Life for the Old," *Journal of Discipleship and Family Ministry* 3, no. 2 (spring 2013): 24-35.
2. Arthur Kornhaber, *The Grandparent Solution: How Parents Can Build a Family Team for Practical, Emotional, and Financial Success* (San Francisco: Jossey-Boss, 2004), 33.
3. Brian Gratton and Carole Haber, "Three Phases in the History of American Grandparents: Authority, Burden, Companion," *Generations* 20, no. 1 (1996): 13.
4. Ibid., 7.
5. Philip Silverman and Robert J. Maxwell, "Cross-Cultural Variation in the Status of Old People," in *Old Age in Preindustrial Society*, ed. Peter N. Stearns (New York: Holmes & Meier 1982), 47.
6. Stearns, *Old Age in Preindustrial Society*, 7.
7. "Age Old Intestate," *Harper's Magazine* 162 (May 1931): 715.
8. Ibid., 715.
9. Ibid., 712-13.
10. Ibid., 712-13.
11. Ibid., 717.
12. Steven Ruggles, "The Decline of Intergenerational Coresidence in the United States, 1850-2000," *Am Social Rev.* 72, no. 6 (2007): 964-89.
13. Beth B. Hess, "America's Age Revisited: Who, What, When, and Why?" in *Growing Old in America*, ed. Beth B. Hess (New Brunswick, NJ: Rutgers University Press, 1980), 9.
14. Gratton and Haber, "Three Phases," 12.
15. Blechman, *Leisureville*, 36.

16. Vern Bengtson argues that family relationships across multiple generations are becoming increasingly important in American society. Vern L. Bengtson, "Beyond the Nuclear Family: The Increasing Importance of Multigenerational Bonds," *Journal of Marriage and Family* 63, no. 1 (2001): 2. In 2012, over 40 percent of children were born out of wedlock and record numbers of couples are divorced every year. Due to the high number of single parent homes, grandparents fulfill family functions such as childcare, financial assistance, and even surrogate parenting. *USA Today* recently reported that multigenerational living is on the rise again and has grown from 3.7 percent of all American homes in 2000 to 5.6 percent of all American homes in 2012. Haya El Nasser, "Multigenerational Homes Increase," *USA Today*, October 12, 2012, sec. A3. The economic needs of previous generations created a mutually symbiotic relationship between generations. The generations needed each other to provide for basic life needs such as food, clothes, and housing. As economic needs continue to increase, it is plausible that the elderly's purpose and place in society will continue to grow in importance.

17. Gratton and Haber, "Three Phases," 13.

18. Arthur Kornhaber and Kenneth L. Woodward, *Grandparents/Grandchildren: The Vital Connection* (Garden City, NY: Anchor /Doubleday, 1981), 131.

CHAPTER 5

The Culture's View of Grandparenting

A Picture of Grandparents Today

Who are grandparents in the twenty-first century? Because grandparents range in age from 30 to 110 and have grandchildren who are babies to retirees, there is a wide range of what it looks like to be a grandparent. Society has incorrect stereotypes of grandparents as primarily individuals who are old, outdated, frail, and have lots of free time. For example, one researcher claims, "There is a bit too rosy a picture of grandparents as well: grandparents get older, sick, die, exact an emotional price for their investments."[1] Grandparents do get older, sick, and die; but they are living longer, are healthier, and in many cases, very involved with family.

Due to increased life expectancy, individuals can expect to spend nearly one-half of their lives as grandparents.[2] Approximately 94 percent of older Americans with children are grandparents and it is estimated that 50 percent will become great grandparents.[3] Adults are becoming grandparents at earlier ages and are spending more of their lives in this role than previous generations. Research indicates that the kind of grandparents that individuals become is, in part, dependent on their perceptions of their own grandparents, their parents' attitudes toward grandparents, and the stereotypes of grandparents created by society and the media.[4]

One stereotype of a grandparent is someone who is physically frail and old-fashioned in thought and lifestyle.[5] This perception is not correct.

Approximately one half of grandparents are under the age of sixty and are not members of the elderly population, with the median age between fifty-three and fifty-seven.[6] Research shows that the average grandparent becomes a grandparent at an early age, lives longer than previous generations, is healthier, is financially stable, and has a living spouse.[7] Szinovacz found that nearly one third of grandparents experience grandparenthood "off time," younger than forty or older than sixty.[8] Grandparents are projected to have fewer grandchildren than past generations due to lower birth rates, more working mothers, and delayed marriage of children.[9] Grandparents have the opportunity to invest more in their grandchildren than previous generations because they have more time, greater financial stability, fewer grandchildren, and live longer.

A second stereotype surrounds the amount of time grandparents have and how they use their time. Many grandparents have large amounts of leisure time, but this is only true for a portion of this demographic. Approximately 50 percent of grandparents work, which limits the time available for family and hobbies.[10] In addition, approximately one in ten grandchildren lives with grandparents.[11] The number of grandparents who operate in a surrogate parent role has risen and is often the result of teen pregnancy, divorce in an adult child's life, or death. Research on grandparents as primary caregivers has shifted from helping grandparents cope with the strain of the role to an approach that also looks at the benefits.[12] Not surprisingly, grandparents who operate as a surrogate parent report receiving numerous benefits such as experiencing joy and aging more successfully.[13]

Grandparents are living longer, but many are not using the extra years to invest in family. Due to the low number of active and engaged grandparents, society has found ways to subsidize grandparent investment.[14] In the twenty-first century, parenting advice comes from psychologists, and parental support comes from paid childcare rather than one's parents. Knowledge is found in books rather than old minds and experience comes from educated professionals rather than the lifetime of skills learned by the elderly. Family meals happen at restaurants instead of Sunday dinners at grandmother's home. Roles that have historically been reserved for grandparents have been outsourced to others, which has been one factor limiting the value of the elderly in the home.

Forgotten Members of the Family

God, Marriage, and Family was written as a comprehensive work on the biblical teaching of family.[15] It is meant to be a definitive resource for any and every topic the Bible addresses regarding family. This book covers every topic imaginable, from the purpose of sex, the role of husband and wife, acceptable forms of contraception, and even models of family ministry churches employ today. Yet this valuable resource is virtually silent on grandparenthood. In this volume, only three passing references are made to grandparents (pp. 92, 141, 193) and these speak of grandparents supporting the family due to death or divorce. The Bible has plenty to say to grandparents and about grandparents, yet from resources written for families one would think that is not the case.

Books such as *A Theology for Family Ministry*[16] and *Visionary Parenting*[17] each devote a chapter to grandparenthood. This is a good start, but it is a sad reality that so few books are entirely devoted to grandparenthood by Christian authors. On a popular level, two of the last books to be written were *The Godly Grandparent* (2007)[18] and *Courageous Grandparenting* (2013).[19] On an academic level, *Intergenerational Christian Formation* (2012),[20] *A Vision for the Aging Church* (2011),[21] and an entire edition of *The Journal of Discipleship and Family Ministry* (2013)[22] devoted to intergenerational ministry suggests that the topic is gaining in popularity. Nonetheless, this fact is shocking, considering how many books Christian publishers print on the topic of parenting.

Why has such an important biblical topic been forgotten or ignored by the majority of present-day theologians and publishers? Grandparents are the forgotten members of the family. The limited attention they receive in books on marriage and family confirms this fact, which reveals a marginalized role that grandparents are given and too readily assume.

Marginalization of Grandparents

Americans are blinded and stifled by ageism—attitudes and practices that lead to the devaluing of older adults.[23] Ageism is rampant in a culture that values new things and discards the old. An example of this mindset is seen in the following advice about the role of a grandparent: "Most grandparents' main role consists in filling in with such extras around the edges.

Extras can be a lot of things—extra attention, extra love, stimulation."[24] The use of the words "extras" and "around the edges" reveals what America thinks of the elderly and where their role is located. Ageism compromises a person's ability to honor and respect a grandparent and limits a grandparent's influence on younger generations.

Cherlin and Furstenberg conducted a nationwide study of grandparent roles and found that parents do not consider grandparents to be primary support members, but important backstage figures.[25] The results of this study speak less to the practice of grandparents and more to the marginalized place grandparents hold in American society. Grandparents will have difficulty transmitting values and influencing a grandchild's faith if they are backstage figures. While the culture undervalues and underutilizes older adults, the Bible demands respect for, remembrance of, obedience to, and partnership with older adults. Americans, led by the church, must rediscover the value of grandparenthood on the spiritual and social development of grandchildren and place grandparents in a prominent role of influence.

Not only does society marginalize grandparents, but a high percentage of grandparents have chosen to marginalize themselves. Cherlin and Furstenberg place grandparents into three categories: detached, passive, and active.[26] They found that one out of every two grandparents interacts with their grandchild less than once or twice a month. Of the grandparents surveyed, 26 percent were detached and inactive in their grandchild's life, with only a fleeting or ritual relationship. A strong majority of detached grandparents live over 100 miles away from grandchildren and face a geographical barrier.[27] Detached grandparents often urge children to be self-sufficient and independent which creates an emotional distance between family members, resulting in grandparents being remote figures in their family's life.

Roughly 29 percent of grandparents were identified as being passively involved with family. These grandparents are careful to keep their distance, do not press for additional time with family, often feel burdened by the responsibility of being a grandparent, and are sometimes ambivalent but still feel the role of grandparenthood is rewarding. Passive grandparents have low expectations and limited involvement.

Active grandparents comprised 46 percent of the individuals surveyed by Cherlin and Furstenberg.[28] Active grandparents spend a lot of time with grandchildren, have a positive view of being a grandparent, regularly share their opinions, and gently tell grandchildren when they disprove of a choice or behavior.

Importance of the Grandparent-Grandchild Relationship

The importance of grandparents in the social and spiritual development of children is just beginning to be recognized in the same light as parents and siblings.[29] Researchers agree that grandparents and grandchildren are important to one another. Grandparents are seen as "significant others" who "have a great deal to do with initial development of one's view of life."[30] Current research is beginning to reveal that grandparents have a robust influence in the spiritual lives of grandchildren.[31] Grandparents are viewed as important, but researchers do not know what motivates grandparents to invest in grandchildren. For example, Friedman and Hechter claim that no theory, empirical study, or rationale exists that explains what motivates grandparents to invest in their family.[32]

Researchers agree that it is important for grandparents to spend time with grandchildren; however, there is no consensus regarding how time should be spent. How are grandparents spending time with grandchildren? In a national study, grandparents reported direct involvement with grandchildren in the following ways: joked or kidded with the child (91 percent); gave the child money (82 percent); watched TV with the child (79 percent); talked to the child about when the grandparents were growing up (77 percent); gave the child advice (68 percent); discussed the child's problems (48 percent); went to church or synagogue with the child (43 percent); disciplined the child (39 percent); took a day trip together (38 percent); taught the child a skill or game (28 percent); and helped settle a disagreement between the child and his/her parents (14 percent).[33]

How often does the average grandchild interact with a grandparent? In one study, grandparents reported how often they saw a grandchild in the previous year: almost every day (12 percent); two or three times a week (11 percent); about once a week (15 percent); once or twice a month (20 percent); once every two or three months (13 percent); less often (20 percent); or not at all (9 percent).[34]

A grandparent's greatest influence occurs in consistent, face-to-face interaction with a grandchild. Influence occurs when habits, values, beliefs, traditions, and heritage are handed down from one generation to another, which is difficult to achieve with limited interaction. Copen and Silverstein, in a longitudinal study, confirmed the importance of grandparents—especially grandmothers—as independent conveyers of religious beliefs to their grandchildren, albeit at a magnitude half that of mothers and fathers.[35] Research also identifies grandmothers as "the central grandparent" who maintains family ties.[36] Grandparent influence on grandchildren is clearly reflected in research by Copen and Silverstein:

> The fact that grandparents were measured before some of their grandchildren were even born speaks to a deep, but perhaps unacknowledged, current of religious consistency that runs through generations in the family. This speaks to the legacy that grandmothers in particular leave for their grandchildren and counters the position of some social scientists who declare and decry the decline of the family's influence over the moral development of children.[37]

Grandparents impact the lives of grandchildren. The stories, hugs, summers on the front porch, and of course, freshly baked cookies, are important memories. Learning values and spiritual truths from grandparents are also important. Waldrop et al., found that intergenerational transmission of grandparent roles occurs as younger generations watch older generations.[38] Their research suggests that younger generations learn how to grandparent by watching those who have gone before them. The grandchild who does not have a relationship with living grandparents has lost something of value.

Grandchildren also impact the lives of grandparents. In the past four decades, literature has argued that the grandparent role provides developmental importance for middle-aged and older individuals.[39] It is argued that grandparenthood helps older adults avoid a season of stagnation, provides a sense of purpose, is rewarding, and offers a second chance to correct mistakes made in parenting. One researcher believes, "Our deepest source of satisfaction and our greatest sense of joy and meaning in life" derive from "our family of origin, which I like to call our vital connections."[40]

Grandparenthood is one of the few new roles that become available to a person later in life.[41] When a grandparent assumes the role, it is necessary that they understand what is expected of them and operate accordingly.

Grandparent Role

The early twentieth century experienced a growing number of negative articles about grandparents, including "Grandma Made Johnny Delinquent"[42] and "The Grandmother: A Problem in Child Rearing."[43] Such publications described the negative impact of the grandmother on the raising of grandchildren. Such articles reflected a growing sentiment by Americans that those of old age were a burden rather than a blessing. In this era, Social Security and old age homes sprung up to transfer what was perceived as a burdensome responsibility from family to society.[44]

The traditional role of grandparents, prior to the preindustrial period, was one in which patriarchal control was exercised over younger generations.[45] As society changed, the role was modified, eliminating any significant role for grandparents in the family. Research of grandparents' roles in the 1950s found that friendship and informality in the grandparent and grandchild relationship was more prevalent when the grandparent held little or no authority in the family.[46] An analysis of the role of grandparents in 75 different societies supported the idea that warm and indulgent relationships between grandparents and grandchildren were found when grandparents were separated from family authority.[47] Researchers such as Chrystal Ramirez Barranti believe not much has changed from the 1950s to today. Barranti's research finds that the primary role by which contemporary grandparents function in American society is indulgence and warmth.[48]

The landmark studies of the 1950s slowly caught the attention of scholars and practitioners who became increasingly interested in the significance of grandparenthood and the roles grandparents assume in the lives of grandchildren.[49] Slowly, researchers began to admit that grandparents had the capacity to influence grandchildren, for good or evil. In 1956, Apple recognized some of the positive qualities of grandparent-grandchild attachment and concluded that grandparents had the ability to show affection even if authority over the family was limited.[50]

The 1960s and 1970s launched the golden age of research on grandparenthood. In 1964, Neugarten and Weinstein published the well-known article, "The Changing American Grandparent," which studied varying roles of grandparents and led to greater attention on the impact of multi-generations on the family.[51] The general consensus from scholars is that the Neugarten and Weinstein study set the trajectory and shaped the field.

The 1964 Neugarten and Weinstein study identified several styles of grandparenting: formal, fun seeker, surrogate parent, reservoir of family wisdom, and distant figure.[52] This study found that just over half of the 70 individuals interviewed for the study were comfortable in their role (59 percent for grandmothers and 61 percent for grandfathers). Grandparents valued the role of grandparenthood for various reasons: it was emotionally fulfilling, it provided an opportunity to be a better grandparent than they were as a parent, they could be a resource, and they could live vicariously through their grandchild.

In 1969, Boyd initiated what has been called the "home plate" theory of a grandparent's home.[53] According to Boyd, grandparents are better off outside of the home of the nuclear family. The theory suggests that grandparents provide a place for family gatherings and vacations but should maintain their own home separate from their children and grandchildren.

In 1970, Kahana and Kahana researched the meaning of grandparenthood from a grandchild's point of view and the way a grandchild's perception of grandparents changed as the grandchild grew older.[54] The study of 85 grandchildren found that 4- to 5-year-old grandchildren value grandparents' indulgent qualities, 8- to 9-year-old grandchildren like active grandparents with whom they can have fun, and 11- to 12-year-old grandchildren prefer some distance from grandparents.

In 1976, Robertson interviewed 86 young adults from the ages of 18 to 26 years old who reported having "very favorable attitudes toward grandparents" and "enjoyed being with them or loved them."[55] Grandparents, it was shown, held an important place in the life of older grandchildren. Also in 1976, Wood and Robertson explored the connection between grandparent involvement and life satisfaction.[56] Wood and Robertson found that those who were more involved in the lives of their children and grandchildren tended to have higher levels of life satisfaction.

In 1981, Kornhaber and Woodward identified several roles for grandparents, including mentor, role model, wizard, and nurturer.[57] By 2004, Kornhaber expanded his list to include ancestor, buddy, hero, historian, spiritual guide, student, and teacher.[58] Kornhaber spent an entire chapter in his book to explain the meaning of each role and provide grandparents with his personal blueprint for grandparenthood.[59]

Table 2. Grandparent roles according to Arthur Kornhaber

Ancestor	Grandparents contain a storehouse of information, report family history, and represent an ancient link to the past.
Buddy	Grandparents have a license to be carefree and have fun with grandchildren because they are not responsible for discipline, daily tasks, or 0running the family.
Hero	Grandchildren see grandparents as durable, strong, and have lived long and had adventures in far-off places creating mystery and excitement.
Historian	Grandparents are the living embodiment of generations past and serve as living witnesses to the history of their own times as well.
Mentor	Grandparents are cheerleaders sparking a child's imagination, inspiring dreams, nurturing spirits, and encouraging intellectual growth while giving a sense of self-worth.
Nurturer	Grandparents are a natural safety net providing emotional care, child support, nursing, counseling, respite, and financial support.
Spiritual guide	Grandparents are wired to care for their child's spirit, not to train them religiously or in morality, but to teach life's true meaning of love and wonder and provide the grandchild with a feeling of transcendence that there is more to life than what meets the eye.
Student	Grandparenthood is a work-in-progress and involves learning. Parents are to teach grandparents how to succeed in their role and update them on modern developments such as technology.
Teacher	Grandparents impart general information and skills that they have learned over their lifetime.
Wizard	The grandparent generates a sense of wonder, inspiration, and imagination through "magical" tricks and fantasies. When the roles of wizard, spiritual guide, and nurturer are combined, the result is a shaman, healer, sage, or whatever the culture calls the "medicine" person.

The instinct to grandparent is as natural as the instinct to parent.[60] When a grandchild is born, grandparents feel the need to do something.

Helen Kivnick calls this the role of centrality and believes research has revealed that grandparenting is central to the life of an elderly person. In 1981, Kivnick identified a total of five dimensions by which grandparents define, or prescribe meaning, to grandparenting. In her research Kivnick identifies the meanings of grandparenthood as valued elder, passing on traditions and being valued in that capacity; immortality through clan, patriarchal or matriarchal responsibility and identification with grandchildren; reinvolvement with personal past, grandparents reliving their own earlier lives and identifying with their own grandparents; and indulgence, attitudes of lenience, and extravagance toward grandchildren.[61]

In 1986, Cherlin and Furstenberg spoke of grandparents as "companions" in which grandparents and grandchildren enjoyed spending time together.[62] Bengtson, in 1985, highlighted three symbolic roles grandparents assume in the life of grandchildren: being there, arbitrator, and family history constructor.[63]

In 2003, Reynolds, Wright, and Beale summarized the role of grandparents by grouping grandparents into four categories: limited contact, participatory roles, voluntary caretaking, and involuntary caretaking.[64] Limited contact refers to grandparents who have limited or no contact with grandchildren. There can be a variety of reasons such as working, traveling, retirement activities, deteriorating health, living far away, indifference, or divorce. Participatory roles encompass the wide range of functions and styles that researchers have identified over the past four decades including roles such as teacher, guide, and playmate. Participatory roles are voluntary; therefore, a grandparent may be highly involved or extremely limited. Voluntary caretakers are those who choose to raise grandchildren or babysit and typically find themselves in the role of parent many days each week. Grandparents may find themselves in this role because of death, divorce, or children who have chosen to have dual-income homes. Involuntary caretakers are grandparents who are the primary caretakers for their grandchildren. Literature refers to these individuals as custodial or surrogate parents who usually find themselves in this position with little or no warning. An overview of studies on grandparent typologies can be found in table 3.[65]

Literature on the role of grandparenthood reveals a wide and varying perspective regarding the place and purpose of grandparents. Researchers commonly hold to the conviction that "unlike other primary family roles, there are not explicit norms for grandparenting."[66] The grandparent's role is unique, and it is not clearly understood by society. Clavan referred to grandparenthood as a "roleless role" because of the diversity of grandparent styles and the absence of prescribed obligations and functions.[67] The lack of understanding about a grandparent's place in the home and purpose in society is seen in the wide range of terms used to describe the role of grandparents in literature: watchdog,[68] arbitrator,[69] stress buffer,[70] roots,[71] family anchor,[72] resource person,[73] valued elder,[74] mentor,[75] and surrogate parent.[76]

Table 3. Studies on grandparent typologies

Author	Sample	Major Findings
Albrecht (1954)	700 randomly chosen grandparents	"Pleasure without responsibility" and "Hands-off policy."
Apple (1956)	75 societies	Close, indulgent, and warm relationships fostered by disassociation of grandparent from family authority.
Neugarten and Weinstein (1964)	70 grandparent couples	Five types: 1. Formal: Grandparents follow prescribed role, keep constant interest in child, and maintain demarcated lines between parenting and grandparenting. 2. Fun Seeker: Informality, playfulness and mutuality of satisfaction characterize the relationship. 3. Surrogate Parent: Grandmother identified role assuming caretaking responsibilities for children at initiative of adult daughter. 4. Reservoir of Family Wisdom: Grandfather identified role as dispenser of special skills and resources, and lines of authority between generations clearly marked. 5. Distant Figure: Contact with child is infrequent although the grandparent is benevolent.
Boyd (1969)	70 four-generation families (45 middle class; 25 blue collar)	Valued grandparent role is learned and earned. Proposed "maternal extended parent role" for grandparents.

Table 3. Studies on grandparent typologies (Continued)

Author	Sample	Major Findings
Robertson (1971, 1977)	257 grandparents (125 women, 132 men)	Four types: 1. Apportioned (high personal and high social) 2. Symbolic (low personal and high social) 3. Individualized (high personal and low social) 4. Remote (low personal and low social)
Clavan (1978)	None	"Realistic" and "Idealistic" roles differentiated by functional centrality grandparent held in family. Proposed a "maternal extended role."
Kornhaber and Woodward (1981)	300 grandchildren (5 to 18 years old)	Five roles from the grandchild's perspective: 1. Historian: Grandparents provide historical, cultural, and family sense of history. 2. Mentor: Grandparents offer wisdom, teach children to work with basics of life, and deepen sex role identity. 3. Role model: Provide role model for future role of grandparent, aging, and family relationships. 4. Wizard: Grandparents are magical in children, telling stories, stoking the imagination. 5. Nurturer/Great Parent: Most basic role grandparents play, widening the support system for children.
Kivnick (1982)	286 grandparents (212 women, 74 men)	Five dimensions of grandparenthood, which exist simultaneously. Grandparents derive meaning from all dimensions with different degrees of emphasis at different times. 1. Centrality: The degree to which the role is central to the grandparent's life. 2. Valued elder: Traditional concept of wise and esteemed elder. 3. Indulgence: Attitudes of lenience and tolerance. 4. Immortality through clan: Feelings of immortality through descendants. 5. Reinvolvement with the past: Grandparent-hood as means of life review.

Table 3. Studies on grandparent typologies (Continued)

Author	Sample	Major Findings
Mueller and Elder (2003)	655 grandparents	Five types: 1. Influential (high on all dimensions) 2. Supportive (close relationship, no disciplinary role) 3. Authority-oriented (high on discipline) 4. Passive (no discipline provided) 5. Detached (low on all measures)

A handful of conclusions may be made about research on grandparent role. First, the research on grandparent role is limited to a handful of studies from the past couple of decades, and many of the studies were conducted on relatively small sample sizes. Are these few studies on small numbers of grandparents conclusive enough to apply the results to all grandparents in America?

Second, one of the major errors in contemporary grandparent literature is to give empirical studies authority to dictate the place and purpose of grandparents in the family. For example, Kornhaber and Woodward state, "We went to [grandparents] as apprentices might to master craftsmen, hoping to learn what it takes to be and function as grandparents."[77] Empirical studies of grandparent role from the past fifty years are not meant to be prescriptive, but descriptive. Their purpose is not to instruct grandparent function, but describe the present-day practices of grandparents.

Researchers who believe the role of a grandparent can be learned from empirical studies face the problem of variance. Which list or roles should be accepted and which should be rejected? Studies on grandparent roles are varied. Different researchers arrive at different results. While there is overlap with a limited number of roles, the lists are diverse enough that no consensus can be had.

What is the true role of a grandparent? Who determines that role? Without the authority of Scripture to guide grandparent function, numerous replacement authorities have been suggested. For many grandparents, one's role is determined by oneself. For example, one grandparent states,

"It was time for me to do something and … to do what *I felt* that I was supposed to do."[78] Another grandparent states her philosophy of grandparenthood in the following way: "In some way it is my job to spoil the kids a bit when they are young, listen to them when they are older and do things for them that their parents do not have the time to do."[79] For others, children are the authority on the role of grandparenthood: "The real experts on the aged are children. Only children understand what elders are for, and only they can meet the real need of the aged: the need to be needed."[80]

The meaning of grandparenthood is foundational to all other dimensions of the role. For example, role behavior is an outcome of role meaning. The behaviors of grandparents are directly connected to the belief grandparents hold about the importance and purpose of their role. Noticeably absent from any study is the meaning of grandparenthood from a Judeo-Christian perspective.

Who determines the role of a grandparent? One scholar believes the role of a grandparent is subjective, as there is a wide range of grandparent behavior and "no single, overriding way of enacting the grandparent role."[81] If society determines the role of the grandparent, then it is a moving target, since that role has consistently changed over the past 150 years.[82] If social science determines that role, then it has yet to be defined, as there is no consensus regarding what the role is. The result is that grandparents are left to define the role for themselves and negotiate what the role is on a family-to-family basis.

Role Confusion

In research literature it is not clear what the role and responsibility of grandparents are.[83] Ambiguity and permissiveness surrounding grandparent role is common. Kivnick believes it is hard to measure grandparent role.[84] Cherlin and Furstenberg believe that "there are no clear guidelines on how to be a grandparent."[85] Conroy and Fahey go so far as stating that there is a "cultural crisis" concerning the meaning and purpose of old age.[86] Hagestad writes, "There was a new uncertainty about what it means to be a grandparent. Members of several generations revealed puzzlement over what grandparents are supposed to do."[87] One researcher discovered, "When we probed deeper we discovered that many grandparents simply did not know anymore what was expected of them."[88] Hagestad summarizes the general sentiment of researchers:

> Several of us who have studied grandparents and grandchildren have been puzzled by some seeming paradoxes in our data. On one hand, interviews and questionnaires present an overall impression of grandparents as important forces in the lives of the grandchildren. On the other hand, it is hard to pinpoint what it is that grandparents *do*.[89]

Role confusion is so prevalent that one author made it the title of his book, *What Are Old People For?* The author answers his own question by suggesting that old people exist to reproduce and see that their offspring are fit to reproduce; an evolutionary perspective applied to grandparenthood.[90] According to this author, the parent's and grandparent's job is the well-being of their offspring, which includes the provision of food, shelter, and protection from predators.[91]

Silverstein and Marenco posit that the role of a grandparent changes in meaning as the family unit ages and as grandparents and grandchildren pass into different life stages.[92] They question if it is even possible to know and understand the role of grandparent:

> The elusiveness of the grandparent role highlights a paradox in family sociology: If the grandparent role is noteworthy for the absence of explicit expectations about the ways it can be enacted and the diverse ways it is performed, is it even possible to identify the contours of the role itself? . . . It has been difficult to fully understand the multidimensional and fluid nature of this complex family role.[93]

Arthur Kornhaber, a child and family psychiatrist, developed a model to help everyone understand their role and place in the family. Kornhaber refers to the model as "parents as the central command."[94] Kornhaber believes parents are the center of the family, empowered with authority to manage the entire system and ensure effective communication between the generations. Grandparents are the foundation of the family, and their main role is to "encourage and support us as parents, respect our new generational boundaries, and expand the way they view us ... and of course have a great time with their new grandchild."[95]

Kornhaber's view is supported by others, including Christians. Christian scholars Conroy and Fahey state, "The grandparents' role is in backing up the parents ... and will be one of helping and being supportive."[96] Yet, this begs the question, *what* are grandparents backing up and being supportive of? *If* parents are raising their children in the Lord, as Ephesians 6:4 commands, then grandparents can support the parents in this effort. If parents are not raising children in the Lord, the grandparent cannot support this unbiblical approach to parenting. This conviction is reflected by Carl Muller:

> The Lord has supplied built-in support staff for beleaguered parents! ... Grandparents share the heart cry of parents for the salvation of children, and they have a vital function in supporting parental efforts to raise children in the nurture and admonition of the Lord.[97]

It is key what the grandparent is supporting. The Bible does not call grandparents to blindly support parents in general, but to specifically support parents in bringing up children in the Lord.

Kornhaber refers to the way grandparents function in modern-day families as "the new social contract."[98] Kornhaber's research suggests that families unconsciously operate under the agreement that children will grow up, become independent, move away from family, and start their own family. The impact of the contract on families is summarized well in the following statement:

> This family contract designated the principles of emotional and personal independence, autonomy, and no enmeshment with one's family of origin. As a result, many of us lead disconnected lives. This is exaggerated by increased geographical mobility and economic opportunity (moving to where the jobs are for the young and moving to the sun belt for retired seniors). When children come along, and support is needed, we find ourselves

independent, autonomous, for sure; but also alone, overburdened, and disconnected.[99]

The social contract has amputated the generations from one another and left countless numbers of grandchildren as grand-orphans who do not have a close personal relationship with an elderly person. Without a grandparent present, parents are forced to look to peers, the media, or paid professionals as the source of wisdom and experience. Grandparents have been liberated from close family involvement and are told they are free to rest, relax, and travel. The erroneous philosophy that asserts, "I raised my children and I'm done," must be replaced by a "parenting is permanent" mentality.

Grandparenthood Today

Hagestad wisely recognizes that in a society without any norms, "we should not be surprised to find a variety of grandparenting roles and styles with behavioral expectations regarding grandparenting."[100] Because the role of grandparents is not clearly defined, it became an appendage, unnecessary for the family to function properly or for children to mature spiritually. Grandparents became concerned that too much involvement would lead to interfering with their children's and grandchildren's lives. So while a relationship between grandparent and family still exists, and can be positive, its limitations removed grandparents from the center of family life and placed them on the periphery with a minimal role.

One of the main roles given to grandparents in literature is that of companion. Grandparents are encouraged to spoil grandchildren, tell stories, give hugs, and be permissive.[101] One author says of grandparents, "They're primed for presents."[102] Joe Horrigan, a child psychiatrist, says that grandparents are in a privileged position; they can give the "goodies" without giving the "baddies."[103] Rather than be an authoritative presence, grandparents are encouraged to be an emotional support.[104] Another author states, "Ideally the role of grandparents is positive re-enforcement: giving praise, hugs and kisses, and emotional encouragement."[105] The general consensus among sociologists is that parents are the disciplinarians who monitor a child's behavior and a grandparent's role consists of offering a grandchild "love, adoration, safety, security, learning, and fun."[106] Experts counseled grandparents to "strive for love and friendship rather than demand respect and obedience. Grandparents coddled and cuddled rather than disciplined; they listened affectionately rather than spoke authoritatively."[107]

Society changed its definition of family from institution to companionship and one manifestation of this change is found in children's literature about grandparenthood.[108] A few notable titles of children's books include *Grandmas Are for Giving Tickles* and *Grandpas Are for Finding Worms*. The children's book *What Grandpas and Grandmas Do Best* suggests that grandparents are for playing hide-and-seek, singing a lullaby, building a sandcastle, and playing games. In *Grandma, Grandpa, and Me*, grandparents are to play with, work along-side, and have fun with. Children's literature speaks of a grandparent's role as one of playmate and companion.

Grandparents adjusted their value system based on the place and purpose society gave to the elderly. Values shifted from leaving a family legacy and financial inheritance to a pleasant retirement experience. A bumper sticker occasionally seen on the car of elderly people captures this well: "We're spending our children's inheritance." Instead of investing in future generations, older couples are encouraged to "indulge themselves a little, in travel, little splurges, or whatever makes their last years more enjoyable."[109] Grandparents who have embraced the role of companion often hold to three values: closeness at a distance, pleasure without responsibility, and noninterference in parenting.[110]

The role of a grandparent in America in the twenty-first century is ambiguous, periphery, and is negotiated on a family-by-family, individual-by-individual basis. Grandparents' life expectancy has increased from 50 years in 1900 to almost 80 years in the twenty-first century.[111] The opportunity for grandparents to invest in their grandchildren's lives has never been greater. Despite grandparents' historically unparalleled opportunity to be involved in their grandchildren's lives, the impact of their investments may have never been smaller than it is today.[112]

Factors that Affect Grandparent Role

Researchers generally agree that grandparents have value. However, the actual value derived from the relationship varies based on factors that impact the grandparent. Research that explores the grandparent role recognizes variability within the grandparent-grandchild relationship. Stelle et al., catalogs over fifteen different factors that create variance in grandparent role, such as age and gender of the grandparent, employment status, education level, personality characteristics, economic resources, geographic proximity, sexual orientation, and family dynamics.[113] Researchers have discovered that how a grandparent functions in their role is impacted as these factors change.

Barranti organized factors that impact grandparent function into five categories: (1) *personal variables* such as age, gender, health, and marital status; (2) *economic variables* such as employment status, education level, and economic resources; (3) *family structure factors* such as number of grandchildren, frequency of contact, and importance of family; (4) *social influences* such as frequency of interaction with friends, community ties, and a number of non-family roles; and (5) *experiences* of one's own grandparents and of one's parents as grandparents to their children.[114] Three factors will be explored in further depth: geographic proximity, quality of relationship between parent and grandparent, and divorce of adult children.

Geographic Proximity

Cherlin and Furstenberg determined the single most important factor determining grandparent involvement was geographic proximity to their grandchild.[115] Silverstein and Marenco note that closer proximity to grandchildren increases the opportunity for grandparents to interact with and support grandchildren.[116] Research suggests that close geographic proximity between grandparent and grandchild is critical; without the dimensions of time and place there can be no intimacy.[117] Studies indicate that the quality of the grandparent-grandchild relationship hinges on frequent contact.[118] It is difficult to instill values and share time together in ten-minute phone calls and occasional holiday trips to grandma's house.[119] Living geographically close to a grandchild increases contact, which in turn leads to an improved relationship.

Kornhaber and Woodward's research discovered that grandparents who moved away from their family felt emotionally disconnected from grandchildren, regret their decision due to the loss of relationship with family, and tend to be narcissistic in thought and action.[120] Kornhaber and

Woodward found that grandparents often felt a sense of regret and loss due to moving away from family. One grandparent from their study states,

> I feel kind of exiled now. My business doesn't need me anymore, my family doesn't need me now and I wasn't there when they did. I feel that I've gypped myself. My husband died and now I'm alone. If I had it to do over again, I would never do it. And if anyone ever asks you about it, tell them that moving away and retirement are bunk.[121]

Studies routinely find distance to be the strongest predictor of frequency of contact between grandparent and grandchild.[122] Kornhaber and Woodward conducted research on 300 American grandparent sets, many of which chose to move away from children and grandchildren and retire to a warm climate. The researcher wanted to know the impact of distance on the grandparent-grandchild relationship. Only 15 were intimately involved with their grandchildren.[123] While it is not impossible to develop strong bonds over long distances, it is difficult.

Because of the mobile American society, families often live hundreds of miles from their nearest relative. Families are increasingly disconnected from one another. Parents frequently find themselves living among persons who do not know their children and who choose not to make an effort to get to know them.[124] This lack of multigenerational care in the lives of children creates what authors David Hay and Rebecca Nye call a "threadbare texture of community," which impoverishes the spirit of children.[125] "Kids need grandparents, but they need active grandparents—grandparents who are not satisfied with watching them grow up from some far, distant bleacher."[126] If possible, grandparents should choose to live in close proximity to their family, as nothing can replace their physical presence in the life of their grandchild.

The greatest spiritual impact can be had when grandparents are physically present in the lives of children and grandchildren. Couples who retire to warmer climates hundreds of miles away from family minimize their spiritual impact on future generations. Cloyd refers to these individuals as "runaway grandparents" or the "fun-seeking generation," who have labored to meet a lifetime of responsibilities and move away from family for fun and adventure.[127] When possible, grandparents should seek to live in close proximity to family. Children can invite parents to live close to family and to be more active in their children's lives, while the church can encourage older adults to finish their lives strong and not waste their final years.

Quality of Relationship

The second most important factor was the quality of relationship between the grandparents and the mother of the grandchildren.[128] Grandparents with an intimate relationship with children offered more help during crisis and were less likely to isolate from one another.[129] Not surprisingly, intimacy with a grandchild often occurs when grandparents concentrate on developing a strong relationship with the grandchild's parents. Scholars refer to the middle generation as the "generational bridge" that mediates contact and links the generations.[130] Parents operate as gatekeepers between grandchildren and grandparent, gaining or restricting access.[131]

Emotional closeness between grandparents and their adult children impacts the grandparent-grandchild relationship. Uhlenberg and Hammill observed that relational strains between grandparents and adult children decreased the amount of time grandparents spent with grandchildren.[132] Kahana and Kahana found the attitudes, expectations, and quality of relationship from adult children to aging parents directly impact the grandparent-grandchild relationship.[133] Researchers have also determined that parental feelings toward grandparents are transmitted to grandchildren, and these attitudes remain throughout a grandchild's life.[134] Grandchildren are more likely to spend time with grandparents when adult children report a strong relationship with their parents.

Grandparents would be wise to address expectations of adult children regarding their role as a grandparent. Research confirms grandparents and adult children have a set of role assumptions and relational expectations for one another.[135] The most common expectations from grandparents are frequent contact with grandchildren and gratitude from family members for involvement with grandchildren.[136] Mothers expect support, but in a non-interfering manner.[137] Grandchildren expect grandparents to share family history, practice family traditions, and give gifts.[138]

Expectations and assumptions often exist as non-communicated ideals in a person's mind and become dangerous when they function as the standard by which another family member is held accountable. Because the grandparent role lacks explicit functions as well as clear rights or responsibilities, families would be wise to discuss expectations and clarify assumptions.[139]

Addressing expectations is critical due to the roles assigned by society to each member of the family. A social contract attempts to define the form and function of a grandparent's role:

> It is social because it is based on attitudes which have been learned and digested from family experience in a changing society. It is contractual because it assumes that parents can and should decide whether—and to what extent—grandparents will nurture their grandchildren. And it is new because it has developed within the lifespan of the current generation of grandparents.[140]

The social contract is a climate of opinion discernable in conversations and patterns of family activity. The contract suggests rather than commands, yet it defines the perceived role of grandparents and creates social mores that are highly regarded and rarely breached. The basis of the contract is not mutual support, but mutual independence where family members embrace the idea that "they have their lives and we have ours."[141] Kornhaber and Woodward describe the mindset of the contract when they state,

> Under the terms of the social contract, no one is obligated to anyone else. . . . Thus, according to the contract, financial or emotional support equals "meddling." Advice or opinion equals "controlling." Interest in lives of the other party equals "interference. . . . The new social contract exists to prevent emotional bonding from taking place."[142]

If Kornhaber and Woodward are correct, America has created social norms for grandparents that are in opposition to what God has designed. Grandparents are being fed a counterfeit role that fails to deliver on its promises and results in isolation not intimacy, separation instead of spiritual influence, and loneliness as opposed to a lasting legacy.

Copen and Silverstein's research revealed stronger relational bonds between grandparent and parent enhanced the spiritual influence of grandparents, especially that of the grandmother.[143] This finding appears to be common sense, yet researchers have confirmed that it is family relationships which tend to be ignored.[144] For grandparents who wish to spiritually influence grandchildren, it is critical to develop and maintain a healthy relationship with all members of the family. Kornhaber offers basic, but often overlooked, guidance when he states, "If we have excellent relationships with grandparents, it is easy to include them on the family team. We only have to ask. If we have past or present difficulties with them, we have to heal any wounds first."[145]

Divorce

Research reveals that grandparent involvement is highest in single-mother families. When a family is affected by divorce, grandparents often become surrogate parents, enter into family life, and invest in a significant way. Numerous researchers have found that grandparents are more, not less, involved when adult children divorce.[146] Divorce distress has resulted in the creation of strong bonds between grandparent and grandchild, as grandparents step into a surrogate parent role. Sociologists believe "there is literally no such thing as a 'single parent.' Some third party is always in the background."[147] Because "the job of childrearing is too big for an individual person to do," families with divorce often rely heavily on grandparents.[148]

A surrogate grandparent is a replacement parent and is the fastest-growing group of grandparents in America.[149] Cherlin and Furstenberger suggest that American grandparents operate according to a norm of "non-interference" in the lives of their adult children. Research indicates that this is valid for most two-parent homes, but not for lone mothers who need and value the presence of a second adult figure in the life of their child.[150] Grandparents, specifically grandmothers, become replacement parents and take care of needs that would otherwise have been the father's role. Grandparents often adopt the role for specific periods of time due to special circumstances (such as a single parent becoming sick) and then return to a secondary role.[151]

When a divorced parent remarries, this may restrict a grandparent's access to grandchildren—particularly on the paternal side of the family—thereby inhibiting the spiritual influence of grandparents.[152] One researcher states, "Historically, divorce has had negative effects resulting in poor relationships with extended kin."[153] Due to divorce, grandparents often withdraw from grandchildren, or a parent withdraws children from a continued relationship with one set of grandparents.[154] In these cases, grandparents must be especially diligent to build and maintain relationships with their family.

Demographic variables impact grandparent role considerably. Family members should not minimize the importance of geographic proximity, relationship between adult children and grandparents, divorce of adult children, or the many other factors. Grandparents who understand the impact of these factors and intentionally plan accordingly will likely experience greater influence and satisfaction as a grandparent.

Summation

Researchers believe grandparents are important and can strengthen families. However, in literature, role confusion exists. Dunham and Smith summarize this sentiment well: "In general, people want to maintain the ties of family but today, more than ever, they are unsure of how it can be accomplished."[155] Table 4 summarizes the state of grandparents in America.[156]

Table 4. How grandparents in America feel about their place and purpose

Powerless	compared to their grandparents who "knew everything" and unable to tell grandchildren anything they don't already know.
Role-less	after retirement with nothing to do and no one to do anything for.
Disconnected	now that their parents are dead and children no longer need them.
Superannuated	because of living a long, healthy life but not experiencing its benefits due to isolation and being disconnected.
Disoriented	by an unfamiliar reality and no idea what to do.
Replaced	by impersonal institutions, services, and personnel that have emerged to fill the vacuum left by grandparents.

Society cannot change the role of grandparenthood, they can only suggest an alternative. Grandparents can reject the indulgent narrative of the twenty-first century and embrace the role God has given them as his heritage builders. Biblically, grandparents are expected to supply a rich Christian heritage for their grandchildren by transmitting faith in Christ, doctrinal beliefs, the fear of the Lord, godly values, and Christ-like conduct to future generations.

The Bible has much to say about the spiritual influence that may be had during the later years of a person's life. The last third of a person's life does not need to be the least productive. Aging provides opportunity for spiritual impact that other times of life do not provide. The Bible encourages grandparents to be spiritually active in the lives of their grandchildren and to think strategically and multigenerationally about the spiritual formation of grandchildren.

A biblical perspective of grandparenthood not only condemns the marginalization of the elderly, but also empowers grandparents for continued service in the family and church. Older Christians should adopt the attitude of Psalm 71:17-18: "O God, from my youth you have taught me, and I still proclaim your wondrous deeds. So even to old age and gray hairs, O God, do not forsake me, until I proclaim your might to all the generations to come." The challenge, and responsibility, for grandparents is to pass on a godly heritage by teaching the commands of Scripture, telling of the glory of the Lord, and treasuring Jesus with their whole heart.

Notes

1. Debra Friedman and Michael Hechter, "Motivating Grandparent Investment," *Behavioral and Brain Sciences* 33, no. 1 (2010): 24-25.
2. Chrystal C. Ramirez Barranti, "The Grandparent/Grandchild Relationship: Family Resource in an Era of Voluntary Bonds," *Family Relations* 34, no. 3 (1985): 343-52.
3. Charlie Stelle et al., "Grandparenting in the 21st Century: Issues in Diversity in Grandparent-Grandchild Relationships," *Journal of Gerontological Social Work* 53, no. 8 (2010): 682-701.
4. Helen Kivnick *The Meaning of Grandparenthood* (Ann Arbor, MI: UMI Research Press, 1982).
5. Glenda Phillips Reynolds, James V. Wright, and Betty Beale, "The Roles of Grandparents in Educating Today's Children," *Journal of Instructional Psychology* 30 (2003): 316-25.
6. Ibid., 317.
7. Joan Aldous, "New Views of Grandparents in Intergenerational Context," *Journal of Family Issues* 16, no. 1 (1995): 104-22.
8. Maximiliane E. Szinovacz, "Grandparents Today: A Demographic Profile," *The Gerontologist* 38, no. 1 (1998): 37-52.

9. Candace L. Kemp, "The Social Demographic Contours of Contemporary Grandparenthood: Mapping Patterns in Canada and the United States," *Journal of Comparative Studies* 34, no. 2 (2003): 187-213.

10. Elizabeth M. Heywood, "Custodial Grandparents and Their Grandchildren," *Family Journal* 7, no. 4 (1999): 367-71.

11. Rachel Dunifon and Ashish Bajracharya, "The Role of Grandparents in the Lives of Youth," *Journal of Family Issues* 33, no. 9 (2012): 1168-94.

12. Bert Hayslip and Julie H. Patrick, *Custodial Grandparenting: Individual, Cultural and Ethnic Diversity* (New York: Springer, 2006).

13. Joan F. Robertson, "Grandmotherhood: A Study of Role Conceptions," *The Journal of Marriage and the Family* 39, no. 1 (1977): 165-74.

14. Friedman and Hechter, "Motivating Grandparent Investment," 24-25.

15. Andreas J. Köstenberger and David W. Jones, *God, Marriage, and Family: Rebuilding the Biblical Foundation* (Wheaton, IL: Crossway, 2010).

16. Michael Anthony and Michelle Anthony, *A Theology for Family Ministry* (Nashville: B & H, 2011).

17. Rienow, *Visionary Parenting*.

18. Dennis Ellingson and Kit Ellingson, *The Godly Grandparent: Living Faithfully and Influencing your Grandchildren for Christ* (Greeley, CO: CLADACH, 2007).

19. Cavin Harper, *Courageous Grandparenting: Unshakable Faith in a Broken World* (Colorado Springs: Christian Grandparenting Network, 2013).

20. Holly Catterton Allen and Christine Lawton Ross, *Intergenerational Christian Formation* (Downers Grove, IL: InterVarsity, 2012).

21. James M. Houston and Michael Parker, *A Vision for the Aging Church: Renewing Ministry for and by Seniors* (Downers Grove, IL: IVP, 2011).

22. Timothy Paul Jones, "Intergenerational Faithfulness," *The Journal of Discipleship & Family Ministry* 3, no. 2 (2013): 8-35.

23. Beth E. Brown, "Spiritual Formation in Older Adults," in *The Christian Educator's Handbook on Spiritual Formation*, ed. Kenneth O. Gangel and James C. Wilhoit (Grand Rapids: Baker, 1994), 3.

24. Christine E. Gudorf, "How to Be Great Grandparents: The Joys and Challenges of Grandparents Today," *U.S. Catholic* 67 (July 2002): 19.

25. Andrew J. Cherlin and Frank F. Furstenberg, *The New American Grandparent: A Place in the Family, a Life Apart* (Cambridge, MA: Harvard University Press, 1992).

26. Andrew J. Cherlin and Frank F. Furstenberg, "Styles and Strategies of Grandparenting," in *Grandparenthood*, 102.

27. Ibid., 103.

28. Cherlin and Furstenberg, "Styles and Strategies of Grandparenting," 102.

29. Barbara R. Tinsley and Ross D. Parke, "Grandparents as Support and Socialization Agents," in *Beyond the Dyad*, ed. M. Lewis (New York: Plenum, 1984), 161-94.

30. Conroy and Fahey, "Christian Perspectives," 205.

31. Casey Copen and Merril Silverstein, "Transmission of Religious Beliefs across the Generations: Do Grandparents Matter?" *Journal of Comparative Family Studies* 38, no. 4 (2007): 507.

32. Friedman and Hechter, "Motivating Grandparent Investment," 24-25.

33. Cherlin and Furstenberg, *The New American Grandparent*, 80.

34. Ibid., 72.

35. Copen and Silverstein, "Transmission of Religious Beliefs," 506.

36. Desiree Seponski and Denise Lewis, "Caring for and Learning from Each Other: A Grounded Theory Study of Grandmothers and Adult Granddaughters," *Journal of Intergenerational Relationships* 7, no. 4 (2009): 390-410.

37. Copen and Silverstein, "Transmission of Religious Beliefs," 506.

38. Deborah P. Waldrop et al., "Wisdom and Life Experience: How Grandfathers Mentor Their Grandchildren," *Journal of Aging and Identity* 4, no. 1 (1999): 33-46.

39. Bradley J. Fisher, "Successful Aging, Life Satisfaction, and Generativity in Later Life," *International Journal of Aging and Human Development* 41, no. 3 (1995): 239-50.

40. Kornhaber, *The Grandparent Solution*, 10.

41. Boaz Kahana and Eva Kahana, "Theoretical and Research Perspectives on Grandparenthood," *Aging and Human Development* 2, no. 4 (1971): 261-68.

42. Clifford A. Strauss, "Grandma Made Johnny Delinquent," *American Journal of Orthopsychiatry* 13, no. 2 (1943): 343-46.

43. Hermann Vollmer, "The Grandmother: A Problem in Childrearing," *American Journal of Orthopsychiatry* 7, no. 3 (1937): 378-82.

44. For a brief history, see Mulvihill, "A New Way of Life for the Old," 24-35.

45. Ramirez Barranti, "The Grandparent/Grandchild Relationship," 344.

46. Siegfried Frederick Nadel, *The Social Foundations of Social Anthropology* (Glencoe, NY: Free Press, 1951).

47. Dorrian Apple, "The Social Structure of Grandparenthood," *American Anthropologist* 58, no. 4 (1956): 656-63.

48. Ramirez Barranti, "The Grandparent/Grandchild Relationship," 344.

49. Thomas E. Denham and Craig W. Smith, "The Influence of Grandparents on Grandchildren: A Review of the Literature and Resources," *Family Relations* 38, no. 3 (1989): 345.

50. Apple, "The Social Structure of Grandparenthood," 656-63.

51. Bernice L. Neugarten and Karol K. Weinstein, "The Changing American Grandparent," *Journal of Marriage and Family* 26, no. 2 (1964): 199-204.

52. Ibid., 199-204.

53. Peter Boyd, "The Valued Grandparent: A Changing Social Role," in *Living in the Multigenerational Family*, ed. W. Donohue, J. Kornbluh and B. Powers (Ann Arbor, MI: Institute of Gerontology, 1969), 79-111.

54. Boaz Kahana and Eva Kahana, "Grandparenthood from the Perspectives of the Developing Grandchild," *Developmental Psychology* 3, no. 1 (1970): 98-105.

55. Joan F. Robertson, "Significance of Grandparents: Perceptions of Young Adult Grandchildren," *Gerontologist* 16, no. 2 (1976): 137-40.

56. Joan F. Robertson and V. Wood, "The Significance of Grandparenthood," in *Time, Roles, and Self in Old Age*, ed. Jaber F. Gubrium (New York: Human Sciences, 1976), 278-304.

57. Kornhaber and Woodward, *Grandparents/Grandchildren*.

58. Kornhaber, *The Grandparent Solution*, 54.

59. Ibid., 53-63.

60. Kornhaber and Woodward, *Grandparents/Grandchildren*, 56.

61. Helen Kivnick, "Grandparenthood and Mental Health: Meaning, Behavior, and Satisfaction," in *Grandparenthood*, 152.

62. Cherlin and Furstenberg, *The New American Grandparent*.

63. Bengtson and Robertson, *Grandparenthood*, 24.

64. Reynolds, Wright, and Beale, "The Roles of Grandparents," 316-25.

65. Adapted from Barranti, "The Grandparent/Grandchild Relationship," 345.

66. Stelle, "Grandparenting in the 21st Century," 683.

67. Sylvia Clavan, "The Impact of Social Class and Social Trends on the Role of the Grandparent," *Family Coordinator* 27, no. 4 (1978): 351.

68. Lillian E. Troll, "Grandparents: The Family Watchdogs," in *Family Relationships in Later Life*, ed. T. M. Brubaker (Beverly Hills: Sage, 1983), 135-47.

69. Gunhild O. Hagestad, "Problems and Promises in the Social Psychology of Intergenerational Relations," in *Aging: Stability and Change in the Family*, ed. R. Vogel et al. (New York: Academic, 1981), 11-47.

70. Vern L. Bengtson, "Diversity and Symbolism in Grandparents' Role," in *Grandparenthood*, 11-25.

71. Conroy and Fahey, "Christian Perspectives," 203.

72. Sarah Harper, "The Challenge for Families of Demographic Ageing," in *Families in Ageing Societies*, ed. Sarah Harper (New York: Oxford University Press, 2004).

73. Neugarten and Weinstein, "The Changing American Grandparent," 199-204.

74. Helen Kivnick, "Grandparenthood: An Overview of Meaning and Mental Health," *Gerontologist* 22, no. 1 (1982): 59-66.

75. Arthur Kornhaber, *Contemporary Grandparenting* (Thousand Oaks, CA: Sage, 1996), 90-91.

76. Neugarten and Weinstein, "The Changing American Grandparent," 199-204.

77. Kornhaber and Woodward, *Grandparents/Grandchildren*, 65.

78. Ibid., 57.

79. Ibid., 68.

80. Ibid., 163.

81. Diane M. Thiele and Thomas A. Whelan, "The Nature and Dimension of the Grandparent Role," *Marriage and Family Review* 40, no. 1 (2006): 93-108.

82. Grandparenthood in America has had three distinct phases: authority, burden, and companion. For a brief history, see Mulvihill, "A New Way of Life for the Old."

83. Vivian Wood, "Grandparenthood: An Ambiguous Role," *Generations: Journal of the Western Gerontological Society* 22 (1982): 18-24.

84. Kivnick, "Grandparenthood and Mental Health,"151.

85. Cherlin and Furstenberg, *The New American Grandparent*, 74.

86. Conroy and Fahey, "Christian Perspectives," 203.

87. Gunhild O. Hagestad, "Continuity and Connectedness," in *Grandparenthood*, 33.

88. Kornhaber and Woodward, *Grandparents/Grandchildren*," 65.

89. Hagestad, "Continuity and Connectedness," 45.

90. William H. Thomas, *What Are Old People For? How Elders Will Save the World* (Acton, MA: VanderWyk & Burnham, 2004), 43.

91. Ibid., 45.

92. Merril Silverstein and Anne Marenco, "How Americans Enact the Grandparent Role across the Family Life Course," *Journal of Family Issues* 22, no. 4 (2001): 493-522.

93. Ibid., 493-94.

94. Kornhaber, *The Grandparent Solution*, 5.

95. Ibid., 5.

96. Conroy and Fahey, "Christian Perspectives," 198.

97. Muller, *Unconverted Sons and Daughters,* 61.

98. Kornhaber, *The Grandparent Solution*, 33.

99. Ibid., 33-34.

100. Hagestad, "Continuity and Connectedness," 36.

101. Steven Bly and Janet Bly, *The Power of a Godly Grandparent: Leaving a Spiritual Legacy* (Kansas City, MO: Beacon Hill, 2003), 16.

102. Ibid., 19.

103. Betty Shannon Cloyd, *Parents & Grandparents as Spiritual Guides* (Nashville: Upper Room, 2000), 85.

104. Emotional support is a role often assigned to grandparents in literature. Arthur Kornhaber has written an entire chapter on how and when to ask for emotional support from grandparents. Kornhaber suggests that a critical role for grandparents is to help during "times fraught with emotional pressures that may tax parents severely." Such times include adoption, divorce, illness, a child with special needs or disability, and adolescence. It has been argued that due to reduced family size, altered expectations, and weakening community ties, nuclear families have become intense emotional environments. Grandparents operate as a moderating force and mediators between the generations helping to soften the intensity that may exist in some families. See Kornhaber, *The Grandparent Solution*, 185.

105. Cloyd, *Parents & Grandparents as Spiritual Guides*, 85.

106. Kornhaber, *The Grandparent Solution*, 50.

107. Gratton and Haber, "Three Phases," 13.

108. Bengtson, "Beyond the Nuclear Family," 1.

109. Carol Shammas, Marylynn Salmon, and Michel Dahlin, *Inheritance in America: From Colonial Times to the Present* (New Brunswick, NJ: Rutgers University Press, 1987), 160.

110. Ramirez Barranti, "The Grandparent/Grandchild Relationship," 344.

111. David A. Coall and Ralph Hertwig, "Grandparental Investment: Past, Present, Future," *Behavioral and Brain Sciences* 33 (2010): 2.

112. Ibid., 2.

113. Stelle, "Grandparenting in the 21st Century," 682-701.

114. Barranti, "The Grandparent/Grandchild Relationship," 346.

115. Cherlin and Furstenberg, *The New American Grandparent*, 107.

116. Silverstein and Marenco, "How Americans Enact the Grandparent Role," 493-522.

117. Kornhaber and Woodward, *Grandparents/Grandchildren,* 69.

118. Dunifon and Bajracharya, "The Role of Grandparents," 1172.

119. Denham and Smith, "The Influence of Grandparents," 347.

120. Kornhaber and Woodward, *Grandparents/Grandchildren*, 70-88.

121. Ibid., 87.

122. Peter Uhlenberg and Bradley Hammill, "Frequency of Grandparent Contact with Grandchildren Sets: Six Factors That Make a Difference," *The Gerontologist* 38, no. 3 (1997): 276-85.

123. Kornhaber and Woodward, *Grandparents/Grandchildren,* 100.

124. Cloyd, *Parents & Grandparents as Spiritual Guides,* 13.

125. David Hay and Rebecca Nye, *The Spirit of the Child*, rev. ed. (Philadelphia: Jessica Kingsley, 2006), 143.

126. Bly and Bly, *The Power of a Godly Grandparent,* 20.

127. Cloyd, *Parents & Grandparents as Spiritual Guides*, 89.

128. Cherlin and Furstenberg, *The New American Grandparent*, 16.

129. Colleen L. Johnson, "Grandparenting Options in Divorcing Families: An Anthropological Perspective," in *Grandparenthood*, 81-96.

130. Silverstein and Marenco, "How Americans Enact the Grandparent Role," 493-522.

131. Joan F. Robertson, "Interaction in Three Generation Families, Parents as Mediators: Toward a Theoretical Perspective," *International Journal of Aging and Human Development* 6, no. 2 (1975): 103-10.

132. Uhlenberg and Hammill, "Frequency of Grandparent Contact," 276-85.

133. Kahana and Kahana, "Grandparenthood," 98-105.

134. Barranti, "The Grandparent/Grandchild Relationship," 346.

135. Maximiliane E. Szinovacz, "Research on Grandparenting: Needed Refinements in Concepts, Theories, and Methods," in *Handbook on Grandparenting*, ed. M. E. Szinovacz (Westport, CT: Greenwood, 1998), 257-88.

136. Karen Somary and George Stricker, "Becoming a Grandparent: A Longitudinal Study of Expectations and Early Experiences," *The Gerontologist* 38, no. 1 (1998): 53-61.

137. Jeanne L. Thomas, "The Grandparent Role: A Double Bind," *International Journal of Aging and Human Development* 31, no. 3 (1990): 169-77.

138. Robertson, "Significance of Grandparents," 137-40.

139. Robert Strom and Shirley Strom, "Building a Theory of Grandparent Development," *International Journal of Aging and Human Development* 45, no. 4 (1997): 255-86.

140. Kornhaber and Woodward, *Grandparents/Grandchildren,* 92.

141. Ibid., 97.

142. Ibid., 97.

143. Copen and Silverstein, "Transmission of Religious Beliefs," 506.

144. Denham and Smith, "The Influence of Grandparents," 349.

145. Kornhaber, *The Grandparent Solution*, 9.

146. See Aldous, "New Views of Grandparents"; Cherlin and Furstenberg, "Styles and Strategies of Grandparenting"; Tinsley and Parke, "Grandparents as Support and Socialization Agents."

147. Jennifer Roback Morse, *Love & Economics: It Takes a Family to Raise a Village* (San Marcos: Ruth Institute, 2009), 105.

148. Ibid., 107.

149. Reynolds, Wright, and Beale, "The Roles of Grandparents," 319.
150. Sarah Harper and Iva Ruicheva, "Grandmothers as Replacement Parents and Partners: The Role of Grandmotherhood in Single Parent Families," *Journal of Intergenerational Relationships* 8, no. 3 (2010): 219-33.
151. Ibid., 226.
152. Copen and Silverstein, "Transmission of Religious Beliefs," 499.
153. Barranti, "The Grandparent/Grandchild Relationship," 346.
154. Keren B. Wilson and Michael R. DeShane, "The Legal Rights of Grandparents: A Preliminary Discussion," *The Gerontologist* 22, no. 1 (1982): 67-71.
155. Denham and Smith, "The Influence of Grandparents," 349.
156. Kornhaber and Woodward, *Grandparents/Grandchildren,"* 130.

PART 4:

DISCIPLESHIP METHODS

CHAPTER 6

The Perceived Role of Christian Grandparents

Four Approaches to Grandparenting

What is the perceived role of Christian grandparents? This chapter answers that question by explaining how Christian grandparents define the responsibilities of grandparenthood and what the grandparent believes his or her role is in the life of their grandchild. Through an open-ended interview, I was able to determine the philosophy by which each individual grandparent operates and how this understanding impacts their involvement with grandchildren.

Approximately three out of four Christian grandparents believe something other than the discipleship of grandchildren is more important. The priority, for a high percentage of Christian grandparents, was encouragement, support, or friendship. For the majority of grandparents, these approaches were the end goal rather than a means to intentionally help grandchildren grow spiritually. Numerous grandparents in these three categories spoke about the importance of the spiritual growth of grandchildren; however, it was not reflected in how they operated as a grandparent, revealing the spiritual life of a grandchild was not as important as they claimed. If grandparents were intentional about the spiritual growth of grandchildren, they tended to fall into the discipleship category as the focal point of their role was more than encouragement, support, or friendship.

My study revealed that grandparents who operate as encouraging voices or loving friends had a minimal impact on the spiritual life of grandchildren. Grandparents who believed their role was to support adult children had stronger relationships than the other approaches and tended to be active grandparents; however, the majority of supportive partner grandparents had a limited impact on the faith of grandchildren. The chart below summarizes the four roles Christian grandparents embrace.

Table 5. Perceived roles of Christian grandparents

Perceived Role	Percent of Grand-parents
Encouraging Voice: A cheerleader who loves grandchildren for who they are and the unique gifting they possess. This grandparent sees the positive and desires to bring out the potential in their grandchildren. One who seeks to help a grandchild accomplish goals and has a natural tendency to ask questions and listen.	16%
Supportive Partner: A helping hand with the day-to-day tasks of parenting. This grandparent operates as a co-laborer who comes alongside their adult children in a variety of ways. Oriented toward seeing a need and meeting a need. An agreeable grandparent who reinforces their children's parenting practices and philosophies without interfering.	32%
Loving Friend: A companion whose focus is building a strong relationship with grandchildren and having fun together. Often avoids difficult conversations or disciplinary matters. An activity-oriented grandparent who likes to create memories, communicate affection, and occasionally spoil grandchildren.	28%
Disciple Maker: A mentor who intentionally attempts to pass faith in Christ to future generations. Desires to see their grandchild know Christ and grow in Christ. Seeks to live as a Christ-like example and share godly wisdom with grandchildren.	24%

Grandparents from the sample population often displayed a primary and secondary approach to grandparenthood. For example, three of four grandparents communicated that a portion of their role included support for children and grandchildren. For some grandparents, support was supplemental to a greater purpose. For others, support was the primary purpose. To differentiate one from the other, I relied upon the grandparent's use of specific terminology, direct statements about their primary role, the overall emphasis of the grandparent in the interview, such as how they use time with grandchildren, and the presence or absence of spiritual practices with grandchildren. Table 5 displays the primary role as understood by grandparents.

Grandparent perception of role was discernable through direct statements regarding what the grandparent described as most important or defined as the goal of grandparenthood. Grandparents who used key words such as cheerleader, positive reinforcement, and encourage, were categorized under the perceived role of encouraging voice. Grandparents who utilized phrases such as help, come alongside, and support, were coded under the perceived role of supportive partner. Key words such as fun, spoil, companion, love, good time, and friend, revealed a grandparent who perceived their role to be a loving friend. Grandparents who spoke about their role as discipler, godly mentor, Christ-like example, or used phrases such as spiritual life, heritage, loving the Lord, and spiritual inheritance, were categorized under the perceived role of spiritual mentor.

Perceived Role 1: Encouraging Voice

According to the sample population, my interpretation and analysis, the least common role for an evangelical grandparent is that of encouraging voice. While 36 percent of grandparents communicated a desire to encourage their grandchild in some way, only 16 percent perceived this as their primary role. Grandparents who operate as an encourager view themselves as cheerleaders whose job is to build up their family and reinforce their adult child's philosophy of parenting. Bill stated, "When they make good decisions … we kind of affirm that." Encouraging grandparents value their grandchildren highly and are hopeful their grandchildren will be successful in life.

According to the research, the most common means of encouragement is prayer. When asked how she encourages her grandchildren, Sarah stated, "I guess just the practice of praying." Other means include living as a positive role model or being a positive voice in their life. The study found that encouraging grandparents tend to reinforce the interests of grandchildren rather than direct grandchildren to specific priorities held by the grandparent. Sarah explained her approach to grandparenting with the following statement: "It was their decision that we just encouraged. We just sat back and encouraged them."

Table 6. Encouraging voice

Participant	Description
Jack	I would like to encourage our kiddos to lighten that burden and encourage what they are already doing in their respective families and encourage them to keep their goals through what they are doing. I'm more so a cheerleader I guess. I love to, as the old song went, accentuate the positive. I love positive reinforcement.
Sarah	We just try to encourage them. That is the main thing.
Linda	To be an encourager. To be a listener when they need to talk to somebody. Be a babysitter when necessary. That is a given. Babysitting is a necessity. To remain a constant in their lives.
Arny	Summarize in one word your role as a grandparent? Encourager.
Elmer	I say a cheerleader is the number one thing. Someone who sees the potential and brings out the giftings that these children have. Encourage their vision to great things.... Basically be another personality that is in their court that sees their value and loves them for who they are.
Larry H.	I don't see my role as very significant, in part, because of distance. We pray for our grandchildren daily. We try to be as much of an encouragement to them as we possibly can.
Larry N.	Being an encourager. Parents are busy making sure they do everything right.... When you are a grandparent, you are one step removed from that. We can kind of relax.
Francine	My job is to encourage their parents to do the right thing. To encourage [grandchildren] to do the right thing even if their parents don't do the right things.

Encouraging grandparents often described their relationship with adult children and grandchildren in positive terms, but spoke of limited interaction due to distance, divorce, or busy schedules. Encouraging grandparents still have spiritual desires for grandchildren, but it was not a dominant theme in their interviews. The spiritual contribution made by encouraging grandparents from this study was small. Francine has grandchildren that do not attend church and explained why she will not have a conversation with her son about the matter: "The parents are answerable to God for how they raised their child. I was answerable for how I raised my children, but I am not answerable. I don't feel like I am for my grandchildren. Now my job is to encourage their parents to do the right thing." Francine remains quiet, in part, because she does not believe she is accountable to God for her grandchildren's faith.

Perceived Role 2: Supportive Partner

Three out of every four grandparents, or 76 percent of the sample population, believe their role includes some form of support for their adult children and grandchildren. According to my analysis, 32 percent of grandparents perceive support to be their primary role. Grandparents who operate as supportive partners desire to come alongside their adult children by reinforcing the parent's philosophy of childrearing and sharing tasks associated with raising children. Jack explained how he implements a supportive approach to grandparenting: "Let's check with mom and dad to make sure it is okay with them. To respect parental authority and back up the parents. . . . Any particular rules, when in doubt, we will check with mom and dad to make sure it is okay."

Supportive grandparents recognize that their adult children need help with the day-to-day tasks of parenting. Elmer stated, "Parents like some help with their children. . . . They are willing to drop their children off here while they go and do something." Bill's adult children have a hectic work schedule so he helps in the following ways: "Just going over to their house to be there with one of the kids until they get back. Or picking them up at school or taking them places." For Jack, support means that he watches grandchildren once a week so his daughter can rest or run errands.

Supportive grandparents often spoke of themselves as partners or teammates. Ann described it this way, "Mom and dad and Softa and Poppy work together and are a team and are doing what we can to benefit their lives." For Valerie, support means reinforcing her adult children's messages to grandchildren; she said, "I would want to reinforce or bolster anything that my kids would say."

Grandparents who operate as supportive partners believe it is their job to implement their adult child's parenting philosophy and preferences. Mike summarized the essence of the support role when he stated,

> Whatever they want us to do, we do. Definitely a support role. They are parenting but at the same time we are helping where we can support them. And also make sure we do what they want us to do. If we have a disagreement about something then we talk to them first. If we can't come to a conclusion we do it the way they want.

Table 7. Supportive partner

Participant	Description
George	I don't want to ever do anything to undermine their plan and their approach for their boys. They are doing such a great job, all I want to do is be supportive.
Ann	We do try to come alongside of them, like I am a helpmate to my husband. I try to be that for my son and daughter-in-law. We come alongside of them. Not co-parents. That is not what I am trying to say, but just be there to support.... I realize that parents need help. As grandparents, it is fun to play and spoil, but we need to come alongside them because you don't want the world to take these children over.
Jack	I see my role as supportive of our kids with the theme of, you have the best mommy and daddy in the world. We may not always agree, but they know best.
Don	During that time of the divorce we were supporting him and financially helping him.
Valerie	I'm in a support role and I'm there to help when they need help.... I would say that I would want to reinforce or bolster anything that my kids would say.
Mike	I see our role basically as support. We are not the parents, that is their responsibility. But at the same time, if we have an opportunity to show a good example or express something that will be helpful we will do it.... Whatever they want us to do, we do.
Jim	We support them as much as we can. We don't want to interfere with how our son or daughter-in-law are raising them, but we are always there to give our support and help whenever we can.... My role as a grandfather and my wife as a grandmother, would be primarily to support our children in raising our grandchildren as much as they want us to be involved. In other words, we are not going to force ourselves on them.
Betty	I think my role is supposed to be a support role for my daughter and my son. I think that is what the Bible has talked about for a long time. Passing it on to the next generation.
Donna	My husband and I both view our role as grandparents as supporting roles. Our job is to reinforce what the mom and dad say and teach their children.
Cheryl	I feel like they consider us not half-partners, but they consider us partners in raising their children.... They are well taught the Scriptures and surrounded by biblical worldview in all things that they do. So we don't feel like we are the only ones pouring into them. All we kind of do is support.

Supportive grandparents communicated a desire to help in practical ways and share the weight of parenting. The two most frequently mentioned means of support were babysitting and financial assistance. Jim babysits grandchildren to strengthen his adult children's marriage: "We know that it is important to have a good marital relationship. So we want to try to support them as far as we can there." In addition, 27 percent of the sample population could be classified in some form of supportive surrogate role primarily due to the divorce of an adult child.

Perceived Role 3: Loving Friend

According to analysis of the research, loving friend was the most common approach to grandparenting from the sample population. Twenty-one of the 25 evangelical grandparents, or 84 percent of the sample population, communicated a desire to have fun with, spoil, or develop a loving relationship with a grandchild in some way. Twenty-eight percent of grandparents believe their primary role is to be a loving friend to their grandchild. Arny embraces this approach to grandparenthood: "For the most part, my job is to love on these kids and to spend time with them." Jim summarized his role as a loving friend in the following way: "To love them and be there for them. That to me is the most important thing." Pam explains her focus with her five-year-old granddaughter: "I connect with her more and more as time goes on. We are becoming friends."

Grandparents who operate as loving friends commonly spoke of spoiling grandchildren as a central component to their role. Ann stated, "We like to spoil them, because they are our only grandchildren." Bill stated why he and his wife spoil their grandchildren, "It is just because we care for them. We want them to be happy." Gary recognizes the cultural messages communicated to grandparents, but finds it hard to break free from these expectations; he referred to "the old saying that grandparents are to make the grandchildren happy."

The study revealed that friendship-focused grandparents often limit rules and avoid the discipline of grandchildren. Jack embodies this approach when he said, "I was determined to allow quite a bit of leeway, the way I see it, and quite a bit of freedom." Jim stated, "We are still going to spoil them in certain areas. We are not going to spank our grandchildren." Jim stated why he avoids the correction of his grandchildren: "It's more important to have a good relationship with our children and grandchildren than impose our views on their raising of their children."

According to analysis of the research, grandparents who operate as loving friends are activity-oriented regarding how they approach their time with grandchildren. Linda explained what her involvement as a grandparent looks like: "We go to all the grandparents' days at school ... and go to all the plays or programs." Valerie's approach is similar: "Having an active role in participating in the activities that they would have in school or sports or extracurricular activities."

Friendship-focused grandparents value fun and activities as a means to that end. Pam, referencing her husband, stated, "His M.O. really is to be the fun grandpa. Always messing around and taking them outside and keeping them on their toes." Fun is central to Gail's approach to grandparenting as well: "I am trying to build a playmate relationship with my grandchildren. . . . Fun is very bonding. I want to be bonded with them."

One positive dimension of grandparents who operate as a loving friend is their active involvement in the life of a grandchild. For example, Ann stated, "I was hands-on . . . we did all kinds of things. We loved them and played with them and tried to give them all kinds of experiences." A second positive dimension is the emphasis on developing a strong grandparent-grandchild relationship. Pam's approach to grandparenting focuses on cultivating a strong relationship with her grandchildren: "I always want them to know how much I love them. Of course, I'm always telling them. I want to be like the listener and responder so that they really do know that there is a grandparent that really feels this connection with me."

A small number of grandparents were strategically developing a strong relationship with a grandchild as a means to deliver the gospel. Gary is the best example of this type of grandparent: "Be careful you don't allow yourself to slump into a spoil mode. You want to love them and rightly so. Do love them and do great things for them. Probably the best thing we can do is love them to Jesus." Ann represents many grandparents who profess evangelical faith today as she intellectually knows she has a greater role than being a loving friend, but still operates in this mode: "Grandparents are there to have fun with their grandchildren and spoil. . . . I guess that is what the world tells me. Yet I know I have more of a stronger, deeper relationship with my grandchildren because of what the Bible teaches."

Table 8. Loving friend

Participant	Description
Ann	Grandparents are there to have fun with their grandchildren and spoil [them]. We are not there to raise them or discipline them.
Sarah	I think the outcome is just to mainly show them we care and are interested in them. No real agenda.
Don	It's like a companion type relationship with them. We'll bring them over to the house. They may swim or they may have dinner with us at the house. Those kinds of things and then we take them back.
Pam	I always want them to know how much I love them ... Comfy, cozy love. That is it. That is what I want to get across. Because that speaks volumes to me that there is an accessibility and acceptance that I want them to know.
Jim	We just want to be there to love them as part of the family and spend time with them and interact with them and enjoy the whole growing up process. That to me is the most important thing.
Betty	You don't feel like you have all those responsibilities on you as a grandparent, you feel like you can just enjoy the grandchildren. I feel that a lot. We can just have a good time with them and enjoy them.
Larry H.	I would like them to know that even though I'm a grandfather that I want them to know that I want them to be a friend. I want them to know how much I love them.
Elmer	That's my thing. Fun. We read books. We take walks. We go to their church with them. Go on hikes. We go out to eat sometimes. Then we play puzzles.
Larry N.	We are not responsible for how this ultimately turns out. It is the parents. So we can kind of just be there to encourage and be fun. Always say that grandpa is in charge of fun. Don't expect any discipline here.
Francine	It's about making them feel special and making them feel they are important to you.
Valerie	I'm there to help when they need help and provide a lot of love and fun. Going to Grammy's house is fun time and play time.

Perceived Role 4: Disciple Maker

Only one of every four grandparents, 24 percent of the sample population, believed their primary role as a grandparent was to focus on their grandchild's faith in Christ. Thirteen out of the 25 grandparents communicated a strong desire to spiritually influence their grandchildren, but only six grandparents perceived their grandchild's faith in Jesus to be their top priority. Gary's approach to grandparenting is focused on the faith of his grandchildren: "Your faith is a lifelong experience of growing in the Lord. That's our real motivation in grandparenting." Mike shares this same conviction: "I think for us the eternal aspect is pretty big. We want to make sure we have a godly heritage left for them." Ray devotes his grandparenting efforts to spiritual matters: "I really try to keep pointing them to Jesus and pray for them." Similarly, Gail stated, "I want them to be challenged to grow in their faith because of me."

Disciple-making grandparents talked about sharing wisdom, being a godly example, passing on faith to the next generation, and helping their grandchildren cultivate a love for Christ and the Bible. Patt shared the following text that her seventeen-year-old granddaughter sent her:

> I have learned more about how to be a Christian by watching how you live your life. The way you pursue a life that reflects him in every way, whether that be through your marriage or simply talking to a man in a restaurant. For seventeen years I have watched you share the gospel shamelessly and point our family towards him. In every situation good and bad I have ever been in, you have reminded me that it is not about me and that I serve a God that has a plan for me that ultimately leads to him. The day we spent going around to different landmarks reading that book is what I attribute the beginning of my spiritual journey to. You showed me that following him is all that matters.

Grandparents oriented toward focusing on their grandchild's spiritual life talked about their role as a ministry and referenced themselves as disciple-makers. Arny talked about using the final third of his life to intentionally invest in his grandchildren: "We don't want to be that couple that's walking the shore picking up the seashells. We have a reason for living. That means that our task is not finished." One grandparent moved across the country to live in close proximity to grandchildren so that they could invest spiritually in them. Mike stated, "In order to give input, we need to be around them. That is why we moved."

Table 9. Disciple maker

Participant	Description
Gary	Their spiritual life, that is the most important thing to us. Not their sports or their piano or school work or whatever. Their spiritual life is uppermost in our minds as far as our communication and contact with them.
George	You know, these people who are so selfish and it's all about them: "Hey, I love my grandkids, but I can't wait to give them back." I don't understand that because my desire and my goal is to see these boys grow up to be good Christian men who love the Lord.
Mike	If we became grandparents, we wanted to make sure that we had some input in their lives for the Lord.... That was our impetus in moving from California to Florida. That tells you the state or the purpose of our value of our grandchildren, we value their eternal heritage more than anything.
Patt	I want my grandchildren to know that I love God with all that I am. When I was thinking about that verse, I went to 2 Timothy 1:5 where it said that Paul was saying that what he saw in Timothy was a sincere faith that had been passed on to Timothy by his grandmother Lois and then by his mother. And that is an heirloom. That is something that is not going to get sold, that is not going to get lost, it is not going to get tarnished or stolen, or sold for money. That is something that is the deepest, richest heirloom that we can pass on.
Ron	I would say my job description as a grandparent is to help my grandchildren to grow [into] healthy, Christian adults who will pass that on to the next generation. That is my job.
Ray	I think the Scriptures are clear on that. Psalm 71. There is another Psalm or two where it talks about passing on to the next generation what God has given you. I think it is a very important role. I didn't realize that until later on in my life.... Man, I have a role to play in their lives and they do respond when I get in touch with them.
Gail	I think my primary role is a disciple.... I want to be a spiritual mentor to my grandchildren. I feel very passionate about that. Yet I feel it is not the easiest part of being a grandparent so far. But right now the focus is on developing the kind of relationship that you can use later for mentoring in a more formal sense. I want my grandchildren not only to know Christ, but to grow in Christ.
Cheryl	I think that there is Scriptural understanding of fathers and mothers and grandparents passing on to the next generation seen in the Psalms. Gray hair is valued in the Psalms and spoken of often. I think that God ordains that we take care of our families.

The study revealed that disciple-making grandparents regularly teach grandchildren from the Bible. Betty stated, "I love the opportunity I have to teach my grandchildren about the Lord." One of Cheryl's main focuses as a grandparent centers on the Bible as well: "We need to have grandchildren that are strong believers in your word, and followers of your word, and obedient to your word." Cheryl holds a similar conviction: "I think it is really critical that they hear, and that they see, and observe people that have a godly, biblical worldview."

Disciple-making grandparents regularly spoke of ways they attempt to help their grandchildren grow spiritually. Carolyn shared the following methods:

> We usually take the kids to Sunday school when we are out there. I'll take movies and books and things that really get spiritual things across to them and we will have some good discussions. . . . I am usually on the lookout for devotionals and anything we can use."

Numerous grandparents referenced Scripture passages as the foundation for their role. Francine was one example, "Whatever the verse is in Proverbs or Deuteronomy, I can't remember, just in your daily walk. That is what we try to do." While reading his Bible, Ray came to the realization that he had an important spiritual role in the life of his grandchildren; he said, "That was maybe ten years ago, or fifteen years ago that I began to realize, wow, I can influence them. I have an influence."

Additional Findings

Six additional subthemes connected to the perceived role of grandparents surfaced. The six themes include lack of clarity, parents as examples, role at church, be fruitful and multiply, financial inheritance, and heritage.

Lack of Clarity

Over one third of the sample population communicated a lack of clarity regarding their role as a grandparent. Don stated, "I never saw myself as having any kind of role at all as a grandparent." Ann commented, "Sometimes it is hard to discern between being a grandparent and a parent." Numerous grandparents confessed that they had given little thought to their job as a grandparent and had no plan for passing faith on to future generations. Pam confessed, "When you contacted me about grandparenting, it was like wow, I'm not even thinking about these things." Valerie summarized the sentiments of many grandparents when she stated, "I'm not sure I have a real good vision for that [her role as a grandparent]."

Table 10. Lack of clarity

Participant	Description
Gary	We are not following some kind of ... organized plan that says we should do this, this, this.
Donna	We are figuring it out. Like our four-year-old, she is the guinea pig. How do you grandparent a four-year-old? ... We don't know what we are doing. Flying by the seat of our pants because there really isn't anything.
Valerie	I'm kind of learning while I go. I think I'm trying to wing it. I think in some areas there might be some fuzziness.
Larry H.	I don't see my role as very significant.
Ray	I know I didn't realize and probably don't fully understand the role of grandparents. I didn't realize that until ten years ago.
Bill	Until you called I really hadn't given much thought about what we were actively doing in-depth with the kids.

Parents As Examples

Data from the qualitative interviews suggest that grandparents are looking for guidance on their role as grandparents. The most common source of guidance was their parent's example as grandparents. Grandparents who were satisfied with their parent's role as a grandparent chose to imitate the positive example they observed. More common were negative experiences, which outnumbered positive experiences two-to-one. Descriptions such as "uninvolved" and "hands-off" were used to reference an undesirable grandparent role. One could argue that grandparents from the sample population want to be more involved and hands-on than their parents and grandparents were.

Jim, whose quote is in table 11, grandparents the way he wished his absentee parents would have grandparented his children. For Jim and others, a negative example of grandparenthood served as a powerful motivation not to replicate the bad experience, but to be more loving and involved as grandparents.

Table 11. Parents as examples

Participant	Description
Jim	I guess we look at it from the perspective of how we would have liked our parents to interact with our kids. We would have loved them to be more loving and involved in their lives.... Our parents were almost the complete opposite: "Hands-off, we don't want any role at all."
Arny	We had parents that were a tremendous role model. We are trying to continue that role model.
Valerie	I'm looking back at the experiences I've had with my grandparents, and while it was sporadic because they lived so far away, based on that, I want to be somebody they can come to talk with, like a safe haven.
Ann	I think, for me growing up, my grandparents, one grandmother was out of state and the other grandparents were on the other side of the state of Florida where I live. So I didn't get to see them very often.... I wouldn't say there was a lot of grandparenting.
Mike	I would preface to say that my kids didn't really have [grandparents]. My parents were both alive when my kids were young, but they didn't really provide much input in their lives at all. Both my kids didn't like their grandparents very much.
Pam	All I can judge by is how I felt toward my grandmother. How I viewed her. How I loved her. How I feel she loved me.
Gail	In all honesty, that is what my parents did with us.

Role at Church

Eleven out of the 25 grandparents are completely disconnected from the youngest generation of their church and have no role in their spiritual life. They may greet young people in the hallway of the church, but do nothing to invest spiritually in their life. Out of the entire sample population, only 2 grandparents, less than 10 percent, spoke of their role with the young people of their church as important or enjoyable. Carolyn stated, "We have kind of taken on the role of being in charge of the nursery. We figure we are pretty good at that." Jim, whose son is a youth pastor at the church he attends, stated, "I think it is important for parents and grandparents to be involved in the ministries of the church, especially with youth and children. We are both involved in Awana and children's ministries."

The remainder of grandparents have an indirect or minimal role with the young people of their church. Mike stated, "We try to help with Sunday school, but generally not a lot. Because you are a grandparent, your grandkids are fine, but it's not like you are hanging out with other kids a lot." Arny is teaching children's Sunday school, but confessed, "We are doing junior church right now . . . preparing and getting ready I'm thinking, 'What am I doing? I don't want to do this. I just want to sit in church and worship and enjoy.'"

Table 12. Role at church

Participant	Description
George	We did a lot of things before, but our roles have kind of slipped.
Sarah	As a grandparent we are not doing a lot at our local church because our grandkids are not here.
Don	We have tried to be more part of the 20 percent rather than the 80 percent that go and are part of the audience, the 20 percent that actually do work at the church. But we've been more or less retired, traveling to go different places and see different places and different people. Lately we have not been as active.
Pam	I don't have a role here as a grandparent.
Ron	Probably not much. It's not my place. I don't think the young people want me.
Larry N.	As far as being involved with youth at our church, we are not.
Bill	Not as a grandparent. Not a particular role.
Cheryl	We don't really have a relationship with other children at this church.

Be Fruitful and Multiply

Only three out of the 25 grandparents from the sample population encouraged their children to have grandchildren, suggesting that they do not believe this is part of their role as grandparents. Most grandparents view the decision to have grandchildren as a private matter and none of their business. Elmer summarized this viewpoint when he said, "Oh, that's in their hands. We didn't encourage or discourage. We were laissez-faire there. We let them make their own decisions. But we certainly delight in each one. We welcome them. Privileged to be grandparents."

This finding suggests that grandparents who profess evangelical faith have adopted unwritten cultural rules about noninterference. Specifically, grandparents operate under the belief that adult children are to live an independent life and make decisions on their own, which includes whether or not to have children and how many. Many grandparents did not feel comfortable providing advice unless asked. In general, grandparents feel no responsibility to talk about God's command to be fruitful and multiply and believe it is an individual decision best left to their adult child.

Table 13. Be fruitful and multiply

Participant	Description
Jack	The concept of family planning in a Christian family. I see it as a personal thing.
Sarah	I left that to them. Of course, we had a lot of joy when they did.
Don	We didn't talk about wanting to be grandparents, needing to be grandparents. We always assumed that they would marry and have children, but it wasn't a need of ours.
Mike	To me, that is kind of pushy. I don't think it is any of our business. If you did, great. I don't think they have grandchildren for me. It's their family.
Arny	They would never talk to us about that. It was pretty much their decision.
Jim	I don't think we encouraged them one way or another to either have children or not to.
Donna	Just left it up to them, although they knew very, very clearly that we wanted grandchildren.
Bill	Those were their decisions. They certainly knew we would love to have grandchildren. There was never any pressure.

A grandchild paradox exists in many families. On one hand, a cultural rule prevents parents from encouraging adult children to be fruitful and multiply. On the other hand, parents expect children to have grandchildren despite rarely talking about the subject. Closely connected are assumptions that adult children will have children. The result of unstated assumptions or undefined expectations surrounding the birth of grandchildren led to disappointment for some grandparents. Patt never spoke with her children about having grandchildren and communicated her sadness: "My son, I don't know if he will have children. He knows it breaks our heart.... I guess I assume that, but I don't think we ever have sat down and said now you will have grandchildren, won't you?"

Financial Inheritance

There was a wide spectrum of views regarding a grandparent's financial responsibility to their family. The sample population's response can be summarized in four views: (1) spend now on family, (2) spend now on self, (3) provide a spiritual inheritance, and (4) save for family. Surprisingly, only 2 grandparents referenced the Bible when discussing this topic. Donna paraphrased Proverbs 13:22 in her answer, "Proverbs says a good man leaves an inheritance to his children's children." However, Donna questioned the meaning of this passage: "I've been thinking about this lately. Is it just financial? Maybe not.... It is just money, or is it things, or is it a legacy? Like a solid marriage?"

Grandparents are looking for guidance on this topic. Cheryl, a disciple-making grandparent, confessed, "I don't think we have any overall plan, or guide how to do that." Jim, like Donna and Cheryl, questioned his financial role with his family: "This is a really good question. One that I struggle with. Is it more important to leave them an inheritance or more important to spend the money on them while you are still alive?" In response to his own question, Jim stated,

> We want to support our grandchildren as much as we can. Not the things that they want, but the things that we think they need. A college education. Or a good Christian-based education, we would want to try to help them with that now. I think it would be more important for a grandparent to help provide a Christian education for the grandchildren while the grandparents are alive than it would be to give them an inheritance maybe after they have gone through the public school system and secular college and not have

that influence while you were alive. I think it is more important to spend the money on them during their formative years, to help them grow spiritually, than to leave them money.

Jim operates with a "spend now" view of financial inheritance and made that clear when he stated his philosophy: "It's better to help them now than to give them an inheritance." In total, eight out of the 25 grandparents from the sample population believe it is best to spend their financial inheritance on their family today. The most common ways grandparents use money in a "spend now" philosophy are financial assistance to purchase a car or home, a financial cushion in case of a large unexpected expense, and provision for Christian or college education. Elmer is motivated by a spend now approach due to his desire to bless his family:

We do share a lot, pretty liberally with blessing the grandchildren and the children pretty regularly. But we are not someone that they are regularly depending on financially. This added blessing kind of thing. I don't feel like we have a strong calling to leave a big inheritance."

Grandparents who hold the second view believe they have no financial responsibility to adult children or grandchildren. Donna stated, "We are not thinking about leaving a [financial] inheritance, but a strong, healthy marriage that we can pass on to them." Larry N. said that "I would say slim to none. I spent it all. . . . I don't think either one of us sees an obligation to leave large sums to our offspring. I think a common thing in our generation is that we don't want any of us to be a burden on our grandchildren." Francine stated, "Well, they are in bad luck. We are spending that now." George expects his children to take care of themselves: "I don't think it's that critical. My expectation is that they are going to stand on their own two feet and be successful. And if there is something left, great. If not, oh well."

A small number of grandparents operate according to a third approach: provide a spiritual inheritance. Gail emphatically stated, "We have no expectations for leaving grandchildren a financial inheritance. I don't care. I want to leave my grandchildren a spiritual inheritance." Patt also shared this view: "That is the least of my priorities. I mean, it really is. . . . God is really refining me on what is important."

The fourth view of financial inheritance was the most common view. Thirteen out of the 25 grandparents communicated the desire to provide children or grandchildren with a future financial gift upon the death of the grandparent. Sarah summarized this approach: "We think it is important and we have a trust." Jack confessed a desire to provide a future financial gift, but also an inability to do so: "Well, I would like to do that. Bluntly, I confess we are not in a position right now to do that. Of a number of weak areas I have, that's probably one of them. I should do more."

Table 14. Financial inheritance

Participant	Description
Ann	I pray there is something there for them.
Don	We want to do that. We've got a living trust that we've set up. It's concerning. We are positive they are going to need it.
Linda	My husband feels very strongly about leaving what he can to help them. Just last night we were talking that he needs to do a new will and he wants to divide things three ways between me, Billy, and Brad.
Mike	We absolutely have a little trust started for both of them. It's not a lot right now. But we plan on kicking in to it a little bit. After they are 21 they can use it for a house or whatever.
Pam	Boy, I pray about that one a lot because we don't have a lot financially. It is one of those things I feel pretty powerless about. We work just to pay the bills. We don't have any family that have gone on ahead that had anything to leave us. That is one of my real regular requests that I would not only have some kind of spiritual heritage to leave my kids and grandkids, but also a financial one.
Cheryl	When we are both gone our estate, or whatever it is, will probably be divided between the children and smaller amounts given to grandchildren.
Valerie	It would be nice, if possible we would like to leave an inheritance, but we would primarily leave it to our kids and let them decide for our grandkids.
Gary	If we don't use it all up living and supporting missions, yes there would be an inheritance for our children.

Heritage

Seven out of the 25 grandparents, or 28 percent, stated that they want to pass on a heritage to their grandchildren. Interestingly, it was rare for a grandparent to speak of leaving a legacy; instead, they used the terminology of heritage, heir, and inheritance to reference their role as grandparents. While it was encouraging that many grandparents associated heritage with their role as a grandparent, they were less clear what type of heritage they were attempting to leave. For some, the desire was to pass on a heritage of faith, for others it centered on family history, and for others it revolved around blessing future generations financially. The consistent theme for all grandparents related to heritage was that they had something to pass on, but there was no consensus regarding the content of what is being passed from one generation to the next.

Table 15. Heritage

Participant	Description
Jack	We are thankful for the heritage that we have, with so many different people being good to our kids growing up, elsewhere through the past several years. In turn, if we can say thanks to the Lord and say thanks to others, at least pass it on, we are glad to do so.
Mike	That tells you the state or the purpose of our value of our grandchildren, we value their eternal heritage more than anything.
Patt	That heirloom that we pass is our faith, to our children and our children's children. I mean we talk about that a lot. We pray that faith will be passed. That the gospel will make a difference in the world that we live in and that they live in.
Arny	He has also blessed us enough that we can share our blessings with the kids in terms of helping them out at key points.... I really believe this has become a motto for Karen and I, that the Lord would find us faithful. Not just in our walk with the Lord, but in how we treat the family. To pass on to our children what was passed to us.
Betty	It's so good to be able to give that heritage to them of faith, of true faith. That is one of my greatest joys in being a grandparent.
Larry N.	And to look back to my own grandparents, I see them as a connect to our heritage. The stories of the past.... I guess I mean a sense of belonging. You are not an isolated individual. You are part of a whole family of people.

CHAPTER 7

Discipling Grandchildren

Eight Methods Every Grandparent Can Use

This section of research sought to understand whether or not Christian grandparents were engaged spiritually with grandchildren and which spiritual methods grandparents used to disciple their grandchildren. I summarize the results as eight spiritual practices grandparents utilize to pass faith on to grandchildren, which are summarized in table below. I discovered that many grandparents are not consistently engaged spiritually with their grandchildren. Such a discovery reinforces the need for churches to encourage and equip grandparents for the role God has given them and for resources to help grandparents pass faith on to future generations.

Spiritual Practice 1: Asking Questions

Six out of the 25 grandparents stated that asking questions of grandchildren is a key spiritual practice. Patt uses questions to talk about social issues that have the potential to negatively influence her grandchildren's faith:

> Let's say the issue of homosexuality. Drinking was a big issue with my children. . . . Let's talk about that. Why don't we go to God's word and come back next week, you do your research. Kind of do things like that. That is where I think kids walk away with their faith rock solid. I think as a grandparent that is what I have been able to do with my grandkids.

Table 16. Spiritual practices

Spiritual Practice	Key Tool	Percent of Grand-parents
Asking Questions: A practice used to generate discussion, create spiritual dialogue, build relationships, and understand what grandchildren believe.	Catechism	24%
Blessing: A prayer requesting God's favor rest upon a grandchild.	Spoken blessing	12%
Intentional meals: An opportunity to discuss matters of faith, teach God's Word to grandchildren, pass on family history, and talk about the events of the day.	Family table	12%
Prayer: The practice of praying with or praying for grandchildren. Common prayers include spiritual protection, physical health, salvation, and daily wisdom.	Praying Scripture	100%
Teaching: The practice of mentoring grandchildren by passing on wisdom that has been accumulated through a lifetime of experience. Common teaching topics include life lessons, social skills, manners, godly morals, and biblical truth.	Godly wisdom	52%
Reading and memorizing the Bible: The practice of reading the Bible with grandchildren, memorizing Scripture together, teaching grandchildren to develop spiritual habits, and giving grandchildren their first Bible.	The Bible	48%
Telling God-stories: The practice of telling grandchildren the work of God in their life which includes a grandparent's conversion, God's provision, God's faithfulness, and God's presence in their life.	Personal testimony	36%
Sharing the gospel: The practice of verbally stating the gospel to grandchildren and inviting grandchildren to respond in faith.	Gospel message	24%

Patt communicated that she wished she asked more question of her own children:

> That is the one thing I would do over again. I wish I would have talked about deep spiritual things and I would have let them talk about it and not been afraid. I wish we would have sat more. I was afraid. So it was shut down instead of allowing there to be free and open discussion.

Patt has learned not to fear questions, or difficult topics, and has created the space for serious spiritual dialogue with grandchildren. She uses questions to begin these discussions.

Table 17. Asking questions

Participant	Description
Sarah	I think just asking questions is the main thing. Asking them to share what they are doing.
Jim	That is the approach we take. Ask questions. How are you doing? What are your plans here? Kind of take it a step at a time and walk through it. Instead of sitting here saying you have to do this or do that. We want to hear their side too. We want their input. We want to understand where they are coming from and not push our ways.
Betty	I love the Westminster Confession and I often say to them, "Hey, what's the chief end of man?" Then they will talk back.
Ron	We don't tell them what to do. Do you think that is right? Do you think your attitude is right? When you let a child make their own decisions and it is something like that, if it was blatant, of course I would have to step in as anybody would. I want them to be comfortable coming to me knowing that I'm not going to be in their face.
Elmer	We have asked questions and had discussions. We try to teach them Bible stories. That's how we use our time right now. But we are waiting for them to come back with more in-depth questions to take them to another level of faith in Jesus. We are building a relationship so it will lead to them coming to us when they have spiritual questions.

One set of grandparents has used catechisms with their grandchildren and believe that the question and answer approach is a valuable tool to help grandchildren grow in their faith. Other grandparents use Old Testament festivals to generate spiritual questions and create discussion. Elmer shared how he employs this approach:

We celebrate the Passover as a family.... The whole format of the Passover is to have the children ask questions of the parents.... We just had the most fun this last spring when I would start telling something of the Passover or something of the Bible story. And here, boom, my grandchildren were asking questions and adding to it and it just became such a fun experience and some creative thinking that I didn't think of came out. So we regularly do that and we often celebrate the feast of tabernacles in the fall. We build a booth in the yard and they help me do that. We talk about how we are pilgrims in this world. How it is not our permanent home. We have a home in the future. We do that as we talk about it, sit in there, enjoy the full moon, and sleep in there overnight and talk about the temporariness of life on this earth and the permanence of heaven and what it takes to get there and how we need to trust Jesus as our Savior and guide.

Spiritual Practice 2: Blessing

Only three grandparents from the sample population mentioned a spiritual blessing for their grandchildren. For Gary and Cheryl, blessing their children and grandchildren is a regular part of their routine: "Gary speaks a blessing over them. We do that even when they are here as a family." For Don, a spiritual blessing is something he sees value in, but not something that he practices:

> We toyed with a thought because in the Bible, upon their death, they would leave a blessing for each child. We really prayed about having the wisdom to provide a blessing, write something, for each child. I wish we could look ahead like Jacob or Isaac. They seem like they had a pretty good handle what their kids were gonna do.

Ray, a grandfather in his 80s, has recently incorporated blessings into his regular interactions with grandchildren. Ray explained what a blessing is and how he blesses his grandchildren.

> The other thing I have learned in the last three years is to bless them. I never leave them or even have a conversation on the phone without saying, "the Lord bless you." I think it is important for grandparents and parents to bless their children. There is something, it's not mystical, it's Scriptural. The whole thing of blessings and curses. I feel it is important that I bless them. . . . You just say the word, "the Lord bless you." . . . It means to bring to full potential. . . . That you may have his favor fully on your life. That is how

I feel. I don't want it to become a trite, mechanical thing. I want to say it from my heart and I think the Lord honors that.

Spiritual Practice 3: Intentional Meals

For most grandparents, meals are a missed opportunity to pass faith on to grandchildren. Only three out of 25 grandparents stated that they intentionally use meals to discuss matters of faith or to teach God's Word to grandchildren. Jack admitted, "Sometimes it is tempting to just feed the kids and get it over with." Valerie agreed: "Mealtimes have been a challenge. . . . There hasn't been a whole lot of instruction or interaction." George admitted that if he is not careful "there are certain things that seem a little ritualistic, you have to pray before you eat." George wisely recognized that "if it's not important to me, it's not going to be important to them."

Table 18. Intentional meals

Participant	Description
Jack	I cherish meal time.... I see that as a time that we can all be together, even if for a short time. We can reinforce conversation, getting to know each other and a time around the Lord.
Betty	With dinnertime, a few months ago, I was taking them through the ten commandments. We sit down and eat and I say, let's go over the first commandment and we talk about that for a moment or two. Then we will talk about the second commandment and so on. In that way it was systematic.
Bill	They know when we are around the dinner table, we talk about what we are doing, Bible studies we are doing. I lead a community Bible study. We will talk about recent lessons we had and some point that we thought was really exciting or neat. Something we heard on radio or from a devotional. Things like that. We will often talk around the table about those things.

Numerous grandparents talked about meals being stressful rather than enjoyable and the desire was to get through the meal as quickly as possible. Grandparents who use meals intentionally use them as an opportunity to communicate about the events of the day, pass on family history, or study the Bible.

Spiritual Practice 4: Prayer

One spiritual practice that is important to every grandparent from the sample population was prayer. All 25 grandparents spoke of praying with or praying for grandchildren. Gary stated, "We pray with our grandchildren on the spot so they know they are being covered when they request something." Elmer highly values praying for his grandchildren: "Praying for them is a big area. We pray for them regularly for their health and well-being, protection, and getting along with each other and their family and parents, being responsive to discipline and direction their parents are giving them."

Prayer is a priority for many grandparents. Betty talked about her passion for prayer: "I come from a long line of prayer warriors. And so I've tried to instill that into our grandchildren by saying to them almost daily I'm praying for you." Jack mentioned, "Grandpa is always willing to pray for them. I want them to know that they have a grandma and grandpa who always keep them in our hearts and prayers." Sarah's one piece of advice for a new grandparent was to "remember to keep your dear family in prayer on a regular basis. Tell them that you are praying for them. I think that is the most important." The study revealed that prayer was a practice that local and long distance grandparents utilized with grandchildren.

Many grandparents felt that one of their primary roles was simply to pray for grandchildren. Sarah believes her role is to pray for the salvation of her grandchildren. Larry H. communicated that they "dedicate and bathe them in prayer." Patt chooses a verse for each of her grandchildren and prays that verse over them. The most common times of prayer revolved around meal times and bed times. George mentioned, "We always pray before meals. I couldn't get away with not praying. Because, especially Jude, he would go 'Grandpa, we haven't prayed yet.'" Jack stated, "With the boys we have prayer time with them at bedtime and then at meal times." Ray summarized the sentiments of a majority of grandparents:

> I think one of the most important things is prayer. We pray for our grandchildren individually and together. We meet, my wife and I, every morning and the last thing we do every night is pray for these children. Prayer is vital. I recognize that. Like this older granddaughter, I pray for her. And I know God hears me. Without him, nothing is going to happen.

Table 19. Prayer

Participant	Description
Gary	They all know that we pray for them. They text me and ask me to pray about something for them. So they know that they can come to us with burdens and we will pray with them about whatever it is.
Jack	We pray for them daily, that the Lord would give them wisdom, each one of them at home and at their schools and wherever they are that they would continue to learn to love God, to love people.
Sarah	We ask them what their prayer needs are.... I think it is keeping involved and letting them know we are praying about specific things.
Ann	We pray with them. We pray when we eat, before we go to sleep. That is even at naptime, not just bedtime. They want you to pray with them at naptime. You don't leave the room. If you forget they know. They do, they ask.
Pam	I pray for these kids every day. Dozens of petitions, blessings over them, and protection. That is the big one. Obviously, even if I was with them 24 hours a day, I wouldn't have total control. I recognize that they belong to God. Their lives are in his hands. Their future. Their destiny. All their days were ordained before one of them came to be. I rest in that.
Arny	I would say that we have tried to model with our children our dependence on prayer.... We have made it an important practice for us, that when we are together as a family, to pray. As a family, the adults and the kids together. Definitely when they are leaving, we gather together in the driveway, in a circle, we hold hands and we pray. And they know that is the last thing we will do, is pray.
Betty	The little ten-year-old girl that calls me, we talk a lot about spiritual things. I told her the other day, "Eva, you are grannie's prayer warrior. There are some things I want you to pray about." "Okay grannie, what do you want me to pray about?" I told her what I want her to pray about.
Donna	We pray for them fervently every day. My husband has an hour-plus commute to work. He says that on his way home, he has a special place, that when he drives by this place, he knows it's time to pray for the grandchildren.

Spiritual Practice 5: Teaching

The second most common spiritual practice after prayer was teaching. The data revealed that grandparents desire to teach grandchildren about a wide range of topics such as life lessons, social skills, manners, and morals. Jack watches Hallmark movies with his grandchildren because "they teach good family lessons and model good behavior and good moral teaching and open up some good discussion." Elmer wants to teach his grandchildren life skills and uses gifts and activities as a means to that end. Don emphasized teaching manners: "We try to teach them manners because some of our grandchildren don't seem like they exhibit manners." Mike wants to teach relational skills: "We want to teach them life lessons and how to work with people and social skills." Betty gets frustrated when she cannot teach her grandchildren something that is important to her.

> I think for grandparents my age, we want to mentor because we have accumulated so much information. It is not because of us, but because of what the Lord has taught us through the years. And I want to pass this on. I think the frustration is when I am stifled to do that. But I feel like, and I think most grandparents feel this, they learn some things and they want to share it, and they don't want to intrude, force themselves on their children to be able to convey that information.

Pam, speaking about her desire to teach, said, "I want to interject truth. . . . Being able to play that role . . . I think about it a lot." For Arny, teaching spiritual truths to grandchildren is a priority: "Any time there is an opportunity for a spiritual lesson, we take the time to do it." Other grandparents look for opportunities to guide discussions toward the Bible. Mike shared his approach: "Whenever possible trying to turn the conversation on things that are Scriptural and biblical as opposed to trying to settle arguments in a secular way." Cheryl, the only grandparent to talk about the importance of teaching grandchildren a Christian worldview, summarized her method:

> First of all, that in our home, they know that there is right and wrong . . . and it's bound by how the Lord has instructed us. Their life in our home, and their home, just revolves so much around the church and the Bible. It's a part of who we are, how we act, and how we talk. You have to teach them the right way. When they begin to see other views you have a grounding from which to jump off of.

While many grandparents desire to teach grandchildren the truths of Scripture, it is not happening in a substantial way for most. Instead, grandparents have settled for low levels of integrating the Bible into daily life. For example, one of the primary means Linda uses to pass on her beliefs is by hanging the Ten Commandments and other plaques on the walls of her home. Linda stated, "There are so many things around this house. Like a shepherd and sheep. And a little plaque that says whatever is right, noble, true, think about these things." Jack admitted, "We don't have heavy discussions at their age." Don stated,

> I don't remember sitting down with them saying, this is what I believe. . . . The ones that are in their twenties, the two boys are questioning what their beliefs are. It's almost like they have reached an age where they are no longer accepting the faith of their parents.

Pam admitted that teaching grandchildren biblical truths has been difficult: "I have found any time I tried to make a formal attempt at having a deeper discussion about something spiritual, they are just not there." Bill confessed, "We are not teaching in any planned, developmental kind of way."

Spiritual Practice 6: Reading and Memorizing the Bible

Less than half of grandparents, 12 out of 25, referenced the use of Scripture with grandchildren. Grandparents are utilizing the Bible in the following ways with grandchildren: Scripture memorization (2), reading Bible stories from a children's Bible (5), giving a Bible as a gift (2), and providing devotionals or Christian literature (3).

One noteworthy finding was that when grandparents are reading the Bible with grandchildren it is almost exclusively from a children's story Bible. Ann stated, "We love to read the Bible storybook." Likewise, Francine shared, "We read Bible stories." Jack makes sure that "when they spend the night with us and we put them to bed, it may be a story or two." While many grandparents value their grandchildren learning biblical principles, grandparents rarely read or teach from an actual Bible. Rather than teach from Scripture, grandparents are relying on storybooks, Christian DVDs that teach good values, or resources such as *Adventures in Odyssey* to transfer the core doctrines of the Christian faith to grandchildren. Mike stated, "My wife buys a lot of books for them. Some of the books will be Bible stories and we will read those to them." Arny trains his grandchildren to develop the spiritual habit of reading the Bible:

> I'm going through the Bible this year, the chronological Bible, which is a devotional thing I'm enjoying. We've encouraged our grandson Levi, he's nine, and he is reading through the Bible each night and we were comparing where we were in the Bible.

On an encouraging note, 3 grandparents spoke of helping their grandchildren develop spiritual habits such as memorization of Scripture and developing a daily quiet time with God. In addition, 2 grandparents gave grandchildren their first Bible. Linda shared, "We have bought their first Bibles. We think that is a grandparent thing to get them their first Bibles." Valerie's admission suggests this is an area where pastors can help: "It's kind of hard now because I'm still learning as they grow, I'm learning what I can do with them at this age."

Spiritual Practice 7: Telling God-Stories

One of the key practices grandparents use to pass on faith to future generations is telling grandchildren the work of God in their life. Barbara explained how she does this: "We tell them. We have told them a number of times about our own experiences of coming to faith in Christ. Where we were. How it happened. What difference it made in our lives." Donna, motivated by what she read in Psalms, tells her grandchildren about how God used the doctors to heal their mommy's cleft palate: "I saw in the Scriptures that my responsibility as a grandparent is to share what God has done and his power with the next generation." Larry N. sees it as his responsibility to "share the history of what God has done in our lives and in our parents' lives." Arny tells his grandchildren the wonderful things God has done because he believes this is a biblical command: "We have been studying a lot in the Old Testament and have been reading that it is really important for us to talk about the Lord with them as much as we can." Arny has utilized a unique method to pass on God stories: "We ask one of our children each Christmas to share their story of how the coming of Christ has impacted their life. We want the grandchildren to hear one of their aunts or uncles sharing how Christ has changed their lives."

Table 20. Reading and memorizing the Bible

Participant	Description
Jack	Working with the girls, the older two, in the Awana program going over verses and reading Bible stories. I'd like to do more of that frankly, as they get older.
Arny	We have been trying to give them devotionals. Christian books. Passing on Christian literature to them as well. Encouraging them to be reading and to have a devotion time. Whatever means we can use to help them dive into the Word and to sing, we try to do that.
Carolyn	We have tried to pray with them about things, read as many stories to them as possible, whether they be Bible stories or other things, devotionals that I mentioned. The other thing we have done, which they love, is I have gotten CDs of Focus on the Family's *Adventures in Odyssey*.
Elmer	The younger ones we have given an *Action Bible*. Even before they can read they can get the story and tell the story and then when they learn to read they can read it on their own. It's been a nice tool. We have given them each a gift of the Bible.
Ray	One of the things I try to do, which we did with all our children, is emphasize the need of memorizing Scripture. I got these little packets I use from Navigators. I haven't recently. I have been trying to memorize whole passages. I think it is important.
Cheryl	When they are here by themselves for a gramma and papa date, we try to have an evening Bible reading time, or Bible story time and we pray with them.

Ray has two creative methods to share God stories with his grandchildren. He records key life experiences with God on MP3 and sends them to all his grandchildren: "I take it from Joshua when he passed through the Jordan and they took these rocks and made a memorial. I'm making a memorial. I have an MP3 recorder and I'm recording my life story." Ray also has taught his grandchildren to share their WTs:

One of the things that is big in our family is a WT. It is Psalm 119:18, "Show me some wondrous thing out of thy word." A WT is a wondrous thing. I will say, what is your WT? What is the Lord showing you from the Word? And that challenges them. My wife and I, we do that with one another. What is your WT? We do that with our grandkids.

Table 21. Telling God-stories

Participant	Description
Mike	We have seen God's faithfulness through many things.... As you remind them what God has done in your life, hopefully they find God is faithful in theirs. I want to make sure his faithfulness is remembered through all their life, through the ups and downs.
Patt	We talk about how God is part of all that we do and all that we are. We talk to them about life. We talk to them about church. We talk to them about things that are going on in the world. We look for ways that God has been shown to be more real than their reality.
Betty	My grandmother was the first person we knew about in our ancestry that became a believer and she prayed for us for a number of years, almost thirty years. We tell the grandkids this. I would explain what it was like before I became a believer and say, boy the Lord's grace just came down on me and changed my heart and we are praying that the Lord will do that to you.
Donna	It is Psalm 71:18, "Even when I am old and gray, do not forsake me, my God, till I declare your power to the next generation, your mighty acts to all who are to come." So that is what spurred me on. That I would take those pictures out and show them to Adeline and tell her what God did in her mommy. That is her heritage. It is my job not to keep that to myself but to pass that on.
Elmer	We do tell them about our salvation experience and pray for theirs.
Larry N.	We share the God-stories with them. Times in our lives when God has been very real. It takes belief out of the hypothetical realm and puts it in the real realm just like in the Old Testament. That is why God said, tell this to your children and your grandchildren, when you sit down and when you walk. Our kids know our God stories.
Arny	I love to tell stories. I love to recount things that have happened to us, clearly we see God has his hand. Ebenezer moments.... I think part of being a grandparent is to be a storyteller. Especially stories about how God has been faithful in our lives.
Ray	We have a lot of miracle stories that we are aware of. God's great deliverance while we were in Honduras. These stories in our lives and the connection we have with Christ, I think, has been the main tool. I really feel it is an important role.

Spiritual Practice 8: Sharing the Gospel

Grandparents were asked what they consider to be their role in the salvation of their grandchildren. Grandparents answered in the following way: praying for a grandchild's salvation (8), supporting parents' efforts (4), no role in sharing the gospel (7), or they have verbally shared the gospel with grandchildren (6). Only one out of four grandparents believe they have a responsibility to verbally share the gospel with their grandchildren. Ann stated, "They have heard and been told the gospel many times. I think that is my role, to show them, and to be there for them and to try to plant as many seeds and let God do his miraculous work."

Table 22. Sharing the gospel

Participant	Description
Gary	We did not have anything to do with the salvation, and the process with our grandchild, that I can think of.
Mike	At some point, if the Lord leads, I might ask, have you given your life to Christ and what does that look like? It won't be so much giving them the gospel per se.... I don't think the evangelism part will be huge.
Jim	We are very concerned with the salvation of our grandchildren. I think the primary responsibility there is the parents' and we want to be supportive of the parents as much as we can. We will say prayers with them and do whatever we can to bring them to a saving knowledge of our Lord and Savior.
Ron	My role is to set an example. My role, I want my grandchildren to see someone who is moral, who loves Jesus Christ, who tries to set an example for them. Just set a good example.
Carolyn	We are trying to get them to have as much exposure to the gospel and spiritual things as we can. And praying for them. We have already explained salvation to the two boys. They were asking questions.
Larry H.	As far as the individual sit down, discuss with them their need or the fact of them making a decision for Christ, my sons have all assumed that responsibility for themselves and my daughters-in-law have... It has not been a very common occurrence for them to come and ask me spiritual questions because I really think their dads and moms have done that well.
Cheryl	I think first of all we need to pray for it and ask the Lord to accomplish it. I think we need to speak of it at every opportunity when we are in conversation with them.

Almost half the grandparents from the sample population believed they had no role or a very limited role supporting the work of parents in the salvation of grandchildren. Sarah confessed, "I admit that we really haven't talked about it. There are a couple [of grandchildren] that called us when they became Christians. That is about it." Jack admitted, "Honestly, there hasn't been a lot of the salvation approach from us to them. It's more so backing up and hearing reports from our kiddos." Elmer stated, "We are waiting for them to ask. I don't feel we are going to be pushing that. We don't really have a plan to do that."

Approximately one out of four grandparents are praying, some fervently, for the salvation of grandchildren. Arny stated, "We pray for them that they will come to a saving faith. We want to be with them forever in eternity in heaven. That is the number one priority as grandparents." Donna has a similar approach: "Prayer is number one. We want to pray that she comes to know Jesus as her Lord and Savior."

Spiritual Abdication

One of the noteworthy findings was the high number of grandparents who communicated that they were not actively engaged in spiritual practices with grandchildren because they assumed the church, Christian school, or parents were active on this front.

Don stated that he was happy to let the other sets of grandparents invest spiritually in his grandchildren because they supplied what "we might be lacking." Larry H. confessed, "It's not a regular thing that I do. . . . I don't think I have done as well as I could'a, would'a, should'a. I wished I had done better." When asked why they operated like they do, Mike stated, "I think, we felt in terms of our input, parents are to train their kids up." Carolyn acknowledged her expectation for the church to train her family: "It is so easy as a parent, if you are involved in a church, to think that the church is going to take care of all of this. If they are learning all this in Sunday school. They are learning all this in youth group and you don't do as much. We are a little too ready to let the church do it."

Table 23. Spiritual abdication

Participant	Description
Don	We attended their baptisms and some of the church functions they have. Honestly, we pretty much let the church do the training.
Gary	I would not say we are directly involved in their spiritual growth.
Ann	Their parents are doing a wonderful job. I don't feel like I need to come in and be a replacement. They get it all the time.
Mike	We haven't had them over enough to have family devotions. What we used to do, because the grandkids, they heard a lot of it at church, so what we would do lots of times, we would have a bowl and we would write questions on them. Or we would write, what are you thankful for.... It's a little more kind of down to where they are at that point rather than just reading a Scripture.
Larry H.	We have a reunion we do most every year, not every year, but most. Of course I assume spiritual leadership there and have a prayer time and discuss a biblical principle. But that is about it . . . I guess I kind of felt that my sons would do that well.
Linda	Kelsey went to Community Bible Study with me. I took him with me every Thursday. He got to have a real good early education to know what it meant to be a Christian. He got to know a lot of biblical stories through that. Course I would sing to him a lot. That type of thing when he was little, to keep him biblically aware, so he would not be totally biblically illiterate.
Bill	We are not really so much on the one-on-one and talking about the deeper things of life. That is pretty much their moms and dads.

CHAPTER 8

Comparing Grandparent Roles

Four Differences Worth Recognizing

Does it matter how a grandparent grandparents? Do all four grandparenting approaches lead to similar results? Or are there noticeable differences? This chapter attempts to answer these questions. To determine differences, the data from disciple-making grandparents was compared with the data from non-disciple-making grandparents to identify recurring themes or outcomes. I identified four recognizable differences between disciple-making and non-disciple-making grandparents: the state of relationship with adult children and grandchildren, living proximity to grandchildren, divorce of adult children, and family members wandering from the Lord.

My research revealed that it does matter how grandparents grandparent. All grandparenting approaches are not different roads that lead to the same results. Different approaches lead to different results. For example, supportive partner grandparents tend to live geographically closer to grandchildren than other grandparents. Disciple-making grandparents had a greater probability of having a strong relationship with children and grandchildren and lower likelihood of having a child experience divorce or a grandchild wander from the Lord. The findings of this chapter confirm that God's ways are the best ways and when a grandparent seeks to obey the Lord, generally, the results are positive.

Table 24. Variance Factors

Description	Grandparents with more biblical understanding of their role	Grandparents with less biblical understanding of their role
Number of grandparents	6	19
Grandparents with strong relationship with children and grandchildren	83% (5/6)	52% (10/19)
Grandparents who live under 100 miles from a majority of grandchildren	16% (1/6)	63% (12/19)
Grandparents with a divorced child	16% (1/6)	31% (6/19)
Grandparents with a grandchild or child who has wandered from Jesus	0% (0/6)	26% (5/19)

State of Relationship

Five out of the six grandparents who were classified as disciple-making grandparents described their relationship with family as strong. Disciple-making grandparents only communicated one instance of estrangement, distant children, lack of communication, or relational problems with family, and this one instance was a result of an adult child's divorce. Cheryl stated, "I have a mantra. This idea of spending quality time is a myth. What kids need is quantity of time. And we tried to do that."

Gary described his relationships as "an extremely close-knit family." Ron stated, "My daughter's kids, we are very close." Ray, a disciple-making grandparent, believes that "we have a good relationship. It's very positive. I try to keep my relationship, first and foremost, with my children." Cheryl, a disciple-making grandparent, sees her relationship with family as a means to a greater end and knows she cannot invest spiritually if there are relational problems. Cheryl stated, "That's part of the intentionality, pursuing a relationship with our children, in addition to our grandchildren."

Table 25. State of relationship

Participant	Description
Sarah	We don't have a lot of communication. That is one of the things that I have wished for. I don't get a lot of cards from them or phone calls from them. They don't initiate it as much. I know that is just because they are busy. It has nothing to do with the relationship.
Don	We don't see them that often, even though they live close. But we have a wonderful relationship.... We don't see the grandchildren that much. They are pretty busy. We probably could see them more if we would initiate more.
Betty	With our son, most of the time I don't know what's going on in his life. I don't really know where his heart is. I don't know that part of him.... I do miss really knowing him.
Bill	We love them. They love us. We are not close enough to do a lot of mentoring. But they know our feeling on everything as it relates to church, family, and so forth. I guess they know us through their moms.
Larry H.	We live in a day that I feel everything is drawing and pulling at people for time. As a consequence, especially my older grandchildren, they have all kinds of things going on. I wish I had more time with them.
Valerie	I need to be more outgoing with initiating time with them.

Nine out of the 19 non-disciple-making grandparents communicated dissatisfaction or relationship problems with at least one adult child or grandchild. Bill admitted, "That has been kind of a sad situation for us. We would love to spend more time with them." Sarah stated, "We do have a good relationship with them. It's not as close as we would like." Approximately half of the non-disciple-making grandparents have at least one relationship with an adult child that can be summarized as a distant relationship that lacks closeness. Distant relationships are characterized by low levels of intimacy, limited time spent together, limited communication, and grandparent dissatisfaction.

The difference between disciple-making and non-disciple-making grandparents is significant when looking at the state of relationships. A disciple-making grandparent has a one in six chance of having a distant or estranged relationship with one adult child or grandchild, while a non-disciple-making grandparent has a one in 2 chance. Don, a non-disciple-making grandparent, has a divorced son and described the relationship in the following way, "It is estranged. We don't see his kids much." Betty summarized the disappointment many non-disciple-making grandparents experience: "They are so caught up in their own lives, and one of my problems is sometimes we don't get a response from them." Larry H. stated, "It's a little bit painful, especially those two older children, not to find time for us. . . . I wish it was a little bit different. I wish we spent more time with the older children. Part of it probably is relationship."

Living Proximity

There was no relationship between living proximity and grandparents who perceived their role to be a disciple-making role. I believed the research would reveal disciple-making grandparents living geographically close to adult children and grandchildren as this would enable them to pass faith on to future generations. Data revealed that the majority of grandparents have grandchildren scattered all over the United States, and some overseas, making it difficult to live close to all grandchildren. Only seven out of the 25 grandparents live within one hundred miles of all their grandchildren. This means that long distance grandparenting is a reality for 72 percent of the sample population.

Surprisingly, 12 out of 19, or 63 percent of non-disciple-making grandparents lived within one hundred miles of a majority of grandchildren. It is worth noting that seven out of eight grandparents who perceive their role to be that of supportive partner lived within one hundred miles of a majority of grandchildren. A grandparent who operates as a supportive partner comes alongside their adult children to help with the day-to-day tasks of parenting and assist with daily needs of the family. Unlike other grandparent roles, being a supportive partner cannot happen from a distance. Thus, the majority of non-disciple-making grandparents who lived geographically close to grandchildren operate as supportive partners. Mike's comments summarize this approach to grandparenting:

> We didn't want to only see them once or twice a year; we wanted to make sure that we could help Emily and Patrick, our daughter and son-in-law, with a lot of things and be around the kids. That was

our impetus in moving from California to Florida. That tells you the state or the purpose of our value of our grandchildren.

Divorce of Adult Child

The difference between disciple-making and non-disciple-making grandparents who have at least one divorced adult child was significant. By comparison, one out of the six disciple-making grandparents had a divorced adult child, while six out of the 19 non-disciple-making grandparents had at least one divorced adult child. Disciple-making grandparents lowered the chances of having a divorced child by half, 16 percent as opposed to 31 percent.

The results of divorce on grandparents are significant. Grandparents with divorced children often experience one of two extremes. Either their relationship with the grandchildren is greatly limited or grandparents fulfill a surrogate parent role. Ron's son is divorced and it has resulted in him having no contact with his grandchildren: "There is almost no relationship. There can't be. It's not an easy thing." Ron followed this statement with the question, "How do you navigate that and the pain?" Carolyn is on the other end of the spectrum and has become a replacement parent: "We spend a lot of time with their three kids. We have to be able to discipline and all of that to go with it."

Wandering from the Lord

Disciple-making grandparents reported no known children or grandchildren who were currently wandering from the Lord. While this finding will not be representative of all disciple-making grandparents, it should be comforting to grandparents. Family ministry experts often communicate that high numbers of young people walk away from the Lord. Findings from this study suggest that this is not the experience of disciple-making grandparents.

Five out of the 19 non-disciple-making grandparents have at least one adult child or grandchild who is not walking with the Lord. To compare the difference, non-disciple-making grandparents have a 26 percent greater likelihood of having a child or grandchild wander from the Lord. Larry H.

stated, "This grandson I told you about, he went away from the Lord. He was dabbling in drugs. . . . He is not back with the Lord yet. That is a prayer concern." Donna, in reference to her unbelieving daughter, stated, "I pray fervently that she does not have children. . . . We have to cling to the promises in his Scripture that he can redeem and restore." Don believes most of his grandchildren are not believers: "We are concerned with that. We are concerned with the other five grandchildren that really need the attention and the loving support and are not attending [church] anymore. . . . The teenagers are getting into trouble. The younger ones are just unhappy."

Reccurring Themes

In addition to the differences presented, various identifiable common themes emerged from the data. Each of the prominent themes are introduced next.

Discipline of Grandchildren

Grandparents were not specifically asked about disciplining grandchildren. Thus, it is significant that the topic of discipline was brought up by 13 of the 25 grandparents. Of these grandparents, many talked about struggles with discipline or wondered what their role was in the discipline of grandchildren. It is clear that this is a critical area where grandparents need guidance.

One principle that stood out was the need for grandparent and adult child to clarify expectations for discipline. Jack stated, "I think I can say confidently we are all on the same page as far as knowing what should be done to discipline the children." Numerous grandparents, such as George, stated that their children gave them permission to discipline grandchildren as needed: "Kim got on me for being too lenient. She says, 'Dad you can't let that go.'" Grandparents who spend regular time with grandchildren, such as watching grandchildren one day a week, often discipline grandchildren out of necessity. Carolyn has a surrogate role as a grandparent and stated, "We spend a lot of time with their three kids. We have to be able to discipline and all of that to go with it."

Other grandparents, such as Donna, do not believe discipline is a grandparent's responsibility: "We will never, ever, ever, ever paddle our grandchildren. That is not our job. Those days are over." Donna believes their role is to train their adult children to discipline grandchildren: "That is the one thing we did do, to make them a paddle. We gave them instructions included, Scriptures included, passages from Proverbs about the rod of discipline." Arny stated that his job is to unconditionally love grandkids and let "the parents be the ones that do the parenting and disciplining." Jim felt strongly about the topic of spanking grandchildren, "We are not going to spank our grandchildren. That is up to the parents to handle that kind of stuff. . . . Even if my son asked me to spank them, I wouldn't."

Betty suggested that discipline of grandchildren is a struggle for her. "I struggle with discipline. Since it is not your kid directly, I have to back off." Larry H. disciplined his fourteen-year-old grandson and said, "I think it may have driven a little bit of a wedge between me and him." Ann stated, "My son and daughter-in-law expect my husband and I to discipline the children. My husband, he doesn't really do that, the physical discipline. I'm the one who disciplines them. I have to say that I don't enjoy it." Valerie referred to discipline of grandchildren as the biggest challenge that she is facing right now and wondered, "Do I step in? Do I say something later? I'm always in a quandary."

Impact of Distance

The research suggested that grandparents who lived geographically close to grandchildren had higher levels of satisfaction and spoke of strong relationships with grandchildren, while grandparents who lived a long distance from grandchildren believed the distance made their role as a grandparent more difficult. Gary, a disciple-making grandparent, stated, "The distance is certainly a difficulty. Because you are trying to maintain a relationship on many levels." Sarah admitted that distance makes grandparenting hard and is her greatest challenge: "Right now, it's long distance. We try to see them as often as we can and be involved in their lives. I can tell you, it's hard because they are not here. We do see them at least twice a year. We travel to see them. They come here when they can." Larry H. agreed, "I would say that distance is somewhat problematic in trying to be as engaged as you would like to be."

Generally, the closer grandparents live to grandchildren, the closer the relationship. Ann stated, "I have a close relationship with him [her grandson] because his mother and he, when he was first born, they lived with me for a couple of years when he was little. So we really bonded." George's grandchildren live on the same property, but in a different home from the grandparents. Having his grandchildren living next door has led to an intimate relationship with them. "They live fifty yards away. They think they have three houses. They don't distinguish between refrigerators, freezers, bedrooms. It's their house. They are our boys. We are so lucky. It couldn't be better." George explained what a typical day with his grandchildren was like:

> I see them every day. Multiple times every day. Noah usually comes into my office and works on his homework. Getting away from his brothers. Jude is funny. He will come in the morning. I always have to keep plenty of bagels around. He will have a bagel and cream cheese. He is usually the first one over here. Luke is in and out. It's funny. We have three bedrooms and an office. One of the bedrooms was always designated as the boys' bedroom. Luke or Noah will go into the boys' bedroom and flop on to the bed and they will have an iPad or something and he will be doing something. Or they will be reading. Noah has Bible at his high school. He likes to do his reading in my office.

Interviewees were asked if they would consider moving across the country to be closer to grandchildren. Sarah stated, "Yes, we have considered that and we have prayed a lot about that." Ann did not want to be a grandchild chaser: "Right now, I would say no, because of our age. We are both fifty-five. We still have a lot of working years ahead of us. I can't just chase my children."

Grandparents who live a long distance from grandchildren have found creative ways to build and maintain family relationships. Jim utilizes technology, "The nice thing, with technology, we get to Skype at least once a week with our grandchild in Cleveland." Ron travels to see his grandchildren and intentionally uses his vacation time: "We spend a lot of time with them. When we can, we are going out there in May and we will probably spend a month with them. We will bring them back here and go on some vacations around here."

Practices That Build Relationships

Grandparents have discovered numerous methods to help build and maintain relationships with grandchildren. Gary, a long-distance grandparent, writes letters to his granddaughter in Florida, and talks on the phone regularly: "I learned how to text because that is the only way I can maintain contact with them. And so I text them, probably every week or so, just letting them know I'm here. I'm praying for them."

George has found a unique way to build a relationship with his grandsons: "The last three years I coached Jude in little league." George also picks up and drops off his grandsons from school, which provides an opportunity to talk while they are in the car. In addition, George stated, "Lots of times we will take the boys with us to breakfast Sunday morning. I like to go to breakfast before church. Then Kim and Dave, who like to sleep in, will come and meet us at church." Cheryl likes to spend large chunks of one-on-one time with grandchildren. "We have grammama, papa dates now. . . . We have one child come at a time. And they come, depending upon their age, for anywhere from two to five days."

Numerous grandparents stated that they actively play with grandchildren. Jack had excitement in his voice when he said, "Sometimes we will do a little playing. We will do horsey rides. Piggy back rides. I'll get down on all fours and they will get on my back." Sarah rented a large beach house to get her family together: "Two summers ago, the entire family, that would be seventeen of us, rented a house on the beach in North Carolina and spent a week there." Sarah also stated that she sends Valentine's cards and Christmas gifts by mail to her grandchildren. Arny and his wife like to divide up grandchildren by gender:

Karen spends time, especially with the girls, doing girl-type things, taking the younger ones out to the dollar store or doing knitting projects with them or just general activities. This last weekend one of the boys, Pete, who is fourteen . . . I was just noticing that the skateboards were laying all around in the garage and so I said let's build a rack for those skateboards. We designed a rack and built that in about three hours and put that up on the wall. He was proud of that. I've found that doing things with the guys is a lot of fun. We kind of divvy them up. I'll spend time with the gals too and Karen will spend time with the guys.

Ann, who lives close to some of her grandchildren, has a scheduled gathering every week: "We have family night once a week. My whole family comes for that and we have dinner and just hang out." Don uses technology: "We take a lot of pictures and share back and forth." Linda makes all her grandchildren afghans. Patt feels strongly about being connected with her grandchildren:

> There is no excuse not to be connected with your grandkids today in a personal way. Not there for the whole family. I mean one-on-one. I text my grandson. We joke back and forth. I do know you have to be really intentional. You have to get into their life. Just like anybody else. They are just your family.

Grandparents, if able, like to be active with grandchildren skiing, biking, camping, playing sports, hiking, and fishing. Ron has been intentional with the activities he has chosen: "My daughter's children, I taught them how to shoot. . . . I taught them how to drive." Ron continued, "Everything takes work. I mean, relationships are work. I don't care who it is. It is work. My wife and I have really worked hard to ensure we have good relationships with these children."

Interfering

Grandparents spoke regularly of not wanting to overstep boundaries, step on toes, or interfere with their adult children's decisions. Ann stated, "We don't want to step on anybody's toes or get in the way." Pam stated, "I want to see them and talk to them as much as I can, without interfering too much." Jim is mindful of his interaction with children: "We don't want to interfere with how our son or daughter-in-law are raising them." Betty's sentiments are similar, "We don't want to intrude, but at the same time we care. . . . We have tried very, very hard not to get into our children's business."

Some grandparents were fearful of saying or doing something that could upset their children and lose privileges with grandchildren, so they purposefully avoid conflict or difficult topics. Larry H. stated, "As a grandfather, I don't want to be overstepping. . . . I don't want to impair a relationship there." Valerie admitted that sometimes she has a tendency to remain quiet: "I didn't want to step on their parenting toes and mess everything up." Mike avoids talking about preference issues and parenting styles and only enters into difficult conversations when he sees children or grandchildren breaking commands of the Bible. Mike stated, "We figure the Lord works with people in their hearts. We pray for them. . . . If it is a preference or style thing, we try not to say a whole lot." A recurring theme was the expectation that grandparents are to remain quiet and autonomous unless adult children invite them in and ask for advice. Jim described this phenomenon:

> We don't want to impose. We won't sit there and say, "You know, you really should do it this way." We let them have the freedom to do their own research and do their own learning on how to raise their children. But we are always there to be supportive and to provide our input when asked.

Grandparents from the sample population avoided talking about the following topics, unless invited to by an adult child: how and when to discipline grandchildren, what grandchildren eat, when grandchildren go to bed, parenting styles, marital issues, and finances. Jim, like many grandparents, believes there are relational rules that require they remain silent. Jim stated, "Unless it was something we were adamantly opposed to, thought that it was not what God wanted, we wouldn't say anything."

CHAPTER 9

Research Results

Key Findings of the Study

This research study examined the biblical, historical, and sociological themes of grandparenting in a variety of contexts and provided an overview of the subject that should aid professors and pastors as they seek to better understand Christian grandparenting. In addition, the study explored the perceived roles and accompanying practices that Christian grandparents have utilized to disciple grandchildren. This chapter discusses the significance of the findings as well as the implications for the results. The following list is a summary of the implications derived from an evaluation of the findings:

1. A relationship exists between grandparents who operate as an encouraging voice in grandparent role and spiritual passivity in grandparent practice.
2. Grandparents who operate as supportive partners typically prioritize helping their children with the day-to-day tasks of life rather than passing on faith to grandchildren.
3. Friendship-focused grandparents often lack intentionality with grandchildren and display low levels of responsibility for their grandchild's faith.
4. Grandparents who lacked clarity of role often operated on the periphery of their family and viewed themselves as minor contributors to the life of grandchildren.
5. Among evangelical grandparents, a relationship exists between a positive or negative experience as a grandchild and future grandparent role.

6. Grandparents are notably absent and minimally contributing to the spiritual life of children and youth in evangelical churches.

7. A common occurrence among evangelical grandparents was the lack of engagement in spiritual practices with grandchildren.

8. Many evangelical grandparents desire to teach biblical truths to grandchildren, but struggle to implement this aspiration.

9. Evangelical grandparents often are not verbally sharing the gospel with their grandchild.

10. Among evangelical grandparents, a relationship likely exists between understanding of role and strength of relationship with children and grandchildren.

11. No relationship exists between disciple-making grandparents and living proximity to grandchildren, which suggests that long distance grandparenting is a reality for many families.

12. A clear distinction among disciple-making and non-disciple-making grandparents is evident with regard to the likelihood of a child or grandchild wandering from the Lord or experiencing divorce.

13. Among evangelical grandparents, a common refrain regarding their involvement with children and grandchildren is "we don't want to interfere, overstep, or intrude."

Explanation of Research Findings

A relationship exists between grandparents who operate as an encouraging voice in grandparent role and spiritual passivity in grandparent practice. The study revealed that encouraging grandparents often assume a passive role, which does not translate well when grandchildren need correction or spiritual direction. The encouragement approach to grandparenthood is suited for families where adult children and grandchildren are walking with the Lord and the grandparent can reinforce the grandchild's love for Jesus. This approach to grandparenthood becomes problematic when grandchildren make poor choices, choose poor friends, or are not pursuing Jesus. In general, grandparents who perceive their role as an encouraging voice tend to have a limited impact on their grandchildren's spiritual life.

Grandparents who operate as supportive partners typically prioritize helping their children with the day-to-day tasks of life rather than passing on faith to grandchildren. While supportive grandparents were quick to state the importance of a grandchild's spiritual life, faith formation was often a secondary priority in the day-to-day activities of the grandparent's relationship with their grandchild and was not a dominant theme in their interviews. If adult children are raising their children to know and serve Christ, the supportive partner approach to grandparenthood can be helpful. This approach to grandparenthood becomes problematic if adult children are not raising grandchildren in the nurture and instruction of the Lord.

Friendship-focused grandparents often lack intentionality with grandchildren and display low levels of responsibility for their grandchild's faith. Friendship-focused grandparents communicate a desire to enjoy grandchildren and have a good time. For numerous grandparents, their stated goal was to create memories, have adventures, or communicate love to a grandchild. A grandchild's spiritual life was a secondary concern to a majority of friendship-focused grandparents.

Grandparents who lacked clarity of role often operated on the periphery of their family and viewed themselves as minor contributors to the life of grandchildren. As a result, numerous grandparents communicated feelings of insignificance in the life of their adult children and grandchildren. Many grandparents who lacked clarity regarding their role also lacked focus regarding how they function as grandparents. For example, Bill's approach to grandparenthood has no focal point and lacks intentionality: "Whichever way the wind is blowing, so to speak. Find something that they want to do or we just choose to keep them busy." Donna admitted, "No grandparents that I know share spiritual encouragement. . . . They won't even say, I read this in the Scripture."

Among evangelical grandparents, a relationship exists between a positive or negative experience as a grandchild and future grandparent role. The data suggests that there are grandparents in evangelical contexts who are not taking their grandparenting cues from the Bible, but rather grandparenting as a replication or rejection of their own experiences with grandparenthood. Grandparents who personally experienced absentee or hands-off grandparents often stated a desire not to replicate this same experience for their grandchildren. Grandparents who experienced positive grandparenting, according to their own expectations, often imitated this example as a grandparent. This finding for grandparents suggests they should evaluate their understanding of the role of a grandparent from the Bible to ensure the approach is grounding in God's Word, not based on a past experience.

Grandparents are notably absent and minimally contributing to the spiritual life of children and youth in evangelical churches. In general, grandparents are not engaging with children or youth from their congregation. Only a handful of grandparents from the sample population pursued a hands-on role with young people in their congregation leading to the finding that, by and large, grandparents do not believe it is their role and are not passing their faith on to young people at their church.

A common occurrence among evangelical grandparents was the lack of engagement in spiritual practices with grandchildren. A likely relationship exists between a grandparent's assumption that grandchildren are receiving spiritual training and a grandparent's spiritual practice with grandchildren. The generalized findings indicate that some grandparents are not spiritually investing in grandchildren because they believe someone else is and this negates the need for their active spiritual involvement in a grandchild's life. The research suggested that high numbers of grandparents perceived the spiritual training of grandchildren as someone else's responsibility and operated as a strong spiritual voice only if no other person fulfills this role in the life of grandchildren. In this way, grandparents see themselves as the last line of defense, but not an active part of the day-to-day spiritual growth process. The result for many grandparents was a hands-off spiritual role that abdicated to other influencers.

Many evangelical grandparents desire to teach biblical truths to grandchildren, but struggle to implement this aspiration. While many grandparents desire to teach grandchildren the truths of Scripture, research suggests it is not happening in a substantial way for most. Closely connected was the finding that high numbers of grandparents are not reading the Bible with grandchildren. A general finding is that grandparents have a limited influence on their grandchildren's faith through the use of the Bible. A second finding is that this presents a large opportunity for churches to train grandparents due the number of grandparents who expressed an interest in learning how to teach biblical truth or a general openness to doing so.

It is possible that if grandparents were provided with a vision, given a resource, and encouraged to teach grandchildren the truths of God's Word, that large numbers of grandparents would be active in this way.

Evangelical grandparents often are not verbally sharing the gospel with their grandchild. Overall, grandparents are concerned about the salvation of grandchildren, but the majority of grandparents, approximately 75 percent, have not verbally shared the gospel with grandchildren. High numbers of grandparents pray for their grandchild's salvation. Many grandparents are mindful that their example may help or hinder a grandchild from coming to faith. Yet many of these same grandparents also stated no intention of sharing the gospel with a grandchild as they did not believe this was their role. This finding suggests there is a relationship between the understanding of one's role as a grandparent and the practical application of that role. Therefore, the implication exists that if a grandparent has a better understanding of his or her role according to the Bible, it is more likely to lead to the practical application of sharing the gospel and manifestation of additional spiritual activity with grandchildren.

Among evangelical grandparents, a relationship likely exists between understanding of role and strength of relationship with children and grandchildren. Approximately half of the non-disciple-making grandparents had one or more relationships that could be summarized as distant relationships that lacked closeness. These grandparents often expressed a longing for more time with family, better communication, and stronger relationships. Research suggested that grandparents who operate according to a disciple-maker viewpoint are less likely to experience estrangement, emotionally distant children, or lack of communication with extended family. Disciple-making grandparents often communicated an intentionality to build relationships and spoke about the importance of initiating family gatherings and regular communication with children and grandchildren. The finding is that grandparents with more biblical perceptions of role were less likely to experience relational problems and more likely to describe the relationship with extended family in highly positive terms.

No relationship exists between disciple-making grandparents and living proximity to grandchildren making long distance grandparenting a reality for many families. Only one out of the six disciple-making grandparents lived within one hundred miles of a majority of their grandchildren. An encouraging result of this finding is that disciple-making grandparents found a way to pass faith on to their adult children and grandchildren from a distance. While living in close proximity would certainly aid a grandparent's efforts to pass faith on to future generations, the disciple-making grandparents accomplished their responsibility while not living in the same city or even the same state as their grandchildren. It should also be noted that a recurring theme from the research found that living proximity impacts the depth and quality of relationship between grandchildren and grandparents. Long distance is not insurmountable, but does make it more challenging for grandparents to build a deep relationship and transmit one's faith to grandchildren. For example, Gail, a grandparent whose grandchildren live in Nepal, was asked to share the spiritual practices that she engages in with her grandchildren, and she responded, "I don't think I have a good list of those. Some of that is the distance."

A clear distinction among disciple-making and non-disciple-making grandparents is evident with regard to the likelihood of a child or grandchild wandering from the Lord or experiencing divorce. Research indicated that disciple-making grandparents have fewer children and grandchildren who walk away from the Lord and who get divorced. This implies that disciple-making grandparents have an impact on the choices, behavior, and beliefs of their children and grandchildren. It also implies that grandparents who have limited or no spiritual investment in a grandchild's life are more likely to see that grandchild struggle with their faith and future marriage.

Among evangelical grandparents, a common refrain regarding their involvement with children and grandchildren is "we don't want to interfere, overstep, or intrude." These expressions were often communicated in the context of bad experiences with adult children or fear of saying or doing something that could upset their adult children and result in lost privileges with grandchildren. Grandparents suggested that they purposefully avoided conflict or difficult topics because they did not want to overstep their boundaries. Many grandparents had a difficult time articulating specific boundaries and were foggy regarding what constituted interference and what did not. For many grandparents, interference was simply what upset their adult children and many times this would not be known until after the fact. A lack of clarity regarding boundaries and expectation commonly led to timidity, passivity, and fear from grandparents. The research results implied that limited universal expectations exist for grandparents (other than non-interference), which require a family-by-family negotiation of agreed upon boundaries to occur.

Research Applications

The results of this research should find its way into seminary classes, Sunday school classrooms, pulpits, books, and conferences, all in an effort to encourage grandparents to take seriously their role as disciple-makers who seek to build a godly heritage of future generations. This research contributes three results to the field of Christian education:

First, biblical themes on the topic of grandparenting were identified. These themes will help grandparents understand their role and pass faith on to future generations. From an application standpoint, pastors and educators should not assume that grandparents understand their role from Scripture. The research revealed that only a small percentage of grandparents referenced Scripture as they talked about their role. In general, grandparents did not know what the Bible said about their role as a grandparent, which is problematic, as grandparents who are unclear about the biblical nature of their role are much more likely to operate from a distorted perspective and have diminished effectiveness in the transmission of faith to grandchildren. Pastors should preach on texts that speak to the role of grandparents, while educators should teach the biblical principles to their classes.

It is helpful to remember that only six out of the 25 grandparents identified the discipleship of their grandchild as the primary focus of their grandparenting efforts. Seventy-six percent of evangelical grandparents in this study invest their grandparenting energy into areas that they perceive to be more important than the discipleship of grandchildren. Most grandparents are working hard to be good grandparents, but many are working at the wrong things. Grandparents need help aligning their priorities and practices with biblical principles.

Pastors are well situated to provide a biblical approach to grandparenthood and this research can help toward that end. Grandparents are looking for guidance, but are rarely finding it from the church. For example, Gail mentioned, "I would love anything. I am a fledgling grandparent.

Especially building the kind of relationship that is going to minister to my grandchildren." One of the most shocking findings was the silence of pastors on the topic of grandparenting. Every grandparent from the sample population was asked how their church has equipped them to be a grandparent; not a single grandparent could remember a sermon preached on the subject, and only one could remember a Sunday school class or seminar taught on grandparenthood. It would be unthinkable for a church to ignore the topic of parenting or marriage, but it appears that churches have overlooked the topic of grandparenting. The overarching application is that seminaries and churches need to pay attention to and incorporate grandparenting into curriculum, programming, classrooms, and pulpits.

The final application deals with multiple spiritual practices that grandparents can be encouraged to pursue with grandchildren. On a positive note, grandparents can be applauded for praying for grandchildren and having informal conversations that help grandchildren grow Christ-like character. Grandparents are actively praying for grandchildren as well as seizing many opportunities to teach grandchildren valuable life lessons. Unfortunately, the majority of grandparents are not regularly reading the Bible or sharing the gospel with grandchildren. Grandparents are abdicating or avoiding these critical practices with grandchildren. A great opportunity exists for pastors and educators to teach grandparents how to lead family worship with grandchildren as well as the importance of communicating the gospel to future generations. Grandparents who were not actively engaged in either of these practices assumed that parents, churches, Christian schools, or other sets of grandparents were communicating the truths of God's Word to their grandchildren. Grandparents need to be encouraged to teach the whole counsel of God, centered on the gospel of Christ, and tell grandchildren the glorious deeds of the Lord so that they place their hope in him and build a heritage of faith unto the Lord.

Second, a sociological analysis of grandparenthood in America has been provided, which fills a gap in Christian education literature. Research into the sociological literature reveals confusion regarding the place and purpose of grandparents in today's family, and research into literature on Christian grandparenting found a large void on the subject. Little has been published in the last ten years on the role and practice of Christian grandparents, especially when compared to the volumes that are published on

Christian parenting every year. The majority of what has been published in the last few years are self-published works that the majority of scholars, pastors, and grandparents will not find. There is a need for Christian authors, publishers, and curriculum companies to create resources that grandparents and churches can use to pass faith on to future generations.

One result of this research project suggests that the definition of family ministry should be revised and expanded. The study of precedent literature revealed that many authors define family ministry in nuclear terms with the focal point being a parent's discipleship of children. The result of this narrowed definition of family ministry is a narrowed practice of family ministry that unintentionally excludes grandparents from consideration. Further research is needed, but it appears as if scholars and pastors who exclude grandparents from their definition of family ministry design ministry programming that does not take grandparents into account. One research recommendation includes broadening the definition of family ministry from a singular focus on the nuclear family to include extended family.

For scholars and authors who have contributed to the literature, a shift in paradigm and pragmatics is in order. As the precedent literature demonstrates, some scholars and authors who believe they are promoting and performing family discipleship are in fact presenting a narrowed version. This does not minimize their efforts; it simply encourages them to expand their perspective to include grandparents. Otherwise, uninformed scholars and authors will continue to unintentionally minimize the discipleship role grandparents are given in the Bible. Over the past decades, scholars and authors have adjusted children and youth ministry models to place a greater emphasis on the equipping of parents in the discipleship of young people. Similar adjustments are needed in family ministry models to accommodate the role God has given grandparents. New ministry models are needed that take into account the biblical role of grandparents and practical ways to equip them to pass faith on to future generations.

Third, limited research exists from an evangelical perspective on the perceived role and accompanying practices of grandparents. This research provides insight into how grandparents in evangelical contexts operate and the practical ways grandparents are discipling grandchildren. Christian grandparents represent an underutilized resource that can be leveraged to make substantial contributions to a young person's faith in Christ. In general, scholars and pastors should take seriously the role God has given grandparents in both the church and home and adjust their theology of the family and philosophy of ministry to align with Scripture.

Research revealed that a majority of grandparents from the sample population do not have a clear understanding of their role. Many are influenced by the cultural definition of grandparents and operate on the periphery of their family. For the most part, Christian grandparents want to make a difference, but need a compelling vision of what they are to do with the final third of their life. Pastors, educators, and authors who wish to influence the faith of children can do so by influencing the faith of a grandparent by equipping them with a multigenerational vision for their family and providing practical help to pass faith to future generations. Grandparents also need to be encouraged not to waste the final third of their life with indulgent pursuits, but to see themselves as disciple-makers who have an essential role with their family and church.

Further Research

The study of grandparenthood is a relatively untouched subject in Christian education. Therefore, many opportunities for further research exist. First, an in-depth study of specific Scripture passages, from the perspective of grandparenthood, such as Deuteronomy 4:9 and Psalm 78, would be a welcome addition to this field. Second, a historical study of the place and purpose of grandparents throughout church history would be a valuable contribution. Specifically, what did church fathers say about grandparents and how did they practice grandparenthood themselves? Third, researchers could build upon this study and expand the number of grandparents who are studied to determine if the results of this study are regional, denominational, and universal. Fourth, a study of grandchildren's perceptions of the Christian grandparent role is needed. What role do grandchildren perceive Christian grandparents to have? Fifth, a comparative study of grandchildren who have active Christian grandparents with those who do not could provide rich findings about the vital role grandparents have in the life of grandchildren. Sixth, a best practices study of churches regarding the effective practices they use to train grandparents for family discipleship could be valuable to other churches who are looking to implement a biblical grandparenting ministry. Seventh, grandfathers have been relatively invisible in grandparenting literature. Few studies have addressed a man's experience as a grandfather. Research into the role and practice of Christian grandfathers would also be a valuable contribution to the field.

APPENDIX 1

Interview Questions

The following interview questions served as the guide for the grandparent interviews. I stated the primary objective in each section and asked the questions related to that objective.

1. Let's talk first about your current relationship with your grandchildren. Please describe that for me and be as detailed as you can.

   a. Describe practices in your life that demonstrate the value you place on grandparenting. (Value of grandchildren; significance of grandparenthood)
   b. How important is it to you that your children have grandchildren? (Be fruitful and multiply)
   c. How does your relationship with your children affect your relationship with your grandchildren? (Leave and cleave)
   d. How often do you see your grandchildren and how do you spend your time with them? (Seeking a sense of how the geographic location impacts interaction)

2. Now I would like you to tell me about how you see your role and responsibilities as a grandparent. Same thing, be as detailed as you can.

   a. What do you consider to be your role as a grandparent with your children and grandchildren? (Heritage builder)
   b. What do you consider to be your role as a grandparent at your local church? (Grandparents investing in generations to come; older training younger)

c. What do you consider to be your role as a grandparent in the salvation of your grandchildren? (Biblical use of generations and genealogies)

d. What do you consider to be your role as a grandparent in the spiritual growth of your grandchildren? (Biblical use of generations and genealogies)

e. What do you consider to be your responsibility as a grandparent in leaving a financial inheritance for your grandchildren? (Financial inheritance)

f. What do you consider to be your role as a grandparent with your grandchildren during retirement years? (Live all one's days serving the Lord)

g. If you were asked to create a job description for yourself as a grandparent, what would you include in the job description?

3. Now could you talk about the spiritual practices you engage in with your grandchildren? Be as detailed as you can in this response too.

a. What do you consider to be the most important spiritual practices for you to be doing in your grandchildren's lives? (Teach, tell, treasure) Probes:

i. How have you utilized traditions to pass on faith to your grandchildren?

ii. How have you passed on key beliefs to your grandchildren?

iii. How have you encouraged your grandchildren to obey God?

iv. How have you utilized meal times to pass on faith to grandchildren?

b. Tell me about your devotional practices. Describe how you are trying to pass that on to your grandchildren.

c. Could you tell me some ways your church has equipped you to disciple your grandchildren?

Validation of Research Protocol

Validation of research protocol for Josh Mulvihill

Robin Jeffers
Coordinator, Assessment/Effectiveness
Bellevue College
12/27/14

Summation

After reading both Josh Mulvihill's dissertation prospectus and two pilot interviews, I find the interview prompts appropriate for eliciting information on the actions evangelical grandparents take as expression of their grandparenting role. In addition, the two pilot interviews show Josh Mulvihill functioning appropriately in eliciting that information. Finally, I see revision of the interview prompts as increasing the focus on the information sought in this study. As focus is tightened and interview length remains the same, information gathered in the interviews should be richer.

Detailed Discussion

Before I began working on this validation I proposed three questions appropriate to qualitative research studies:

- Are the interview questions likely to elicit the information the interviewer seeks?
- Is the interviewer operating without bias—not seeking a particular answer?
- Is the interviewer probing appropriately, that is, seeking clarification or further detail?

In order to familiarize myself with the research project and how it's progressed thus far I took three steps, described here in the order they occurred and with the objective/goal of each step:

1. Read both interview transcripts (objective: determine interviewer's interviewing and probing skill)
2. Read prospectus (objectives: gain familiarity with analysis of biblical attitude toward grandparenting, and relate that analysis to the interview questions)
3. Compare interview questions in two ways:
   a. interview 1 to interview 2 (objective: validate consistency in delivery of interview questions)
   b. proposed interview questions to actual interview questions (objective: validate reasoning behind changes in interview questions)

Once I had read the pilot interviews and prospectus I had two more questions:

- Have revisions to the interview protocol improved it?
- Is there information the research proposal seeks that is not showing up in the transcriptions and if so, is it possible to tell why?

Answering these questions has allowed me to identify three key strengths of the interview process:

- The interview questions allow interviewees to describe their actions as evangelical grandparents elicit the information Mr. Mulvihill seeks.

- The interview transcripts show Mr. Mulvihill's consistency and objectivity in delivering the interview questions. He appears not to be injecting bias into the questions. While he is new to probing, it's worth mentioning that interview 2 shows more ease with that technique: interview 1 took just thirty minutes and interview 2 took advantage of the full hour.

- The revision of interview questions described in the prospectus and the revisions that occurred between completion of the prospectus and the pilot interviews show Mr. Mulvihill using his biblical research to reformulate interview questions. Among additions to actual interview questions are probes that get at specific biblical injunctions: inheritance and the guidance to be fruitful and multiply. Other new questions display the same movement to limiting information gathering to that which will enrich his tightly focused study.

I am pleased to recommend that Josh Mulvihill move on to the interview phase of this research.

Robin Jeffers
December 30, 2014

APPENDIX 3

Methodological Design

T his chapter describes the methodology used to explore the practices and perceived roles of Christian grandparents. In addition to a description of the research procedures, this chapter describes the instrumentation used in conjunction with the research method, the population that was examined along with the sampling procedures, and any delimitations this study required. An explanation of the limitations to the generalizations of this study is also described.

Research Question Synopsis

The following questions directed the collection and analysis of data for the proposed research study.

1. What is the grandparent's role in nurturing the faith of future generations according to biblical analysis?
2. What is the perceived role of grandparents in evangelical contexts toward their grandchildren?
3. What are the practices of grandparents in evangelical contexts toward their grandchildren?
4. What variation in grandparent role is influenced by selected demographics (age of grandchild, age of grandparent, number of grandchildren, living proximity to grandchild, divorce, and health of relationship to children)?

Research Design Overview

The first phase, found in chapter 2, examined major biblical themes pertaining to grandparenthood; six themes were identified and studied along with individual Scriptures that apply to grandparents. The methodological design of the second phase of this study explored perceptions of Christian grandparent roles and accompanying family discipleship practices. The second phase was an exploratory study that other researchers may build upon in future studies. The study was descriptive in nature.

Table 1A. US Census information on the five states

State	Total Population	Older Adults	% of Total Population
CA	37,353,956	4,246,514	11.4
FL	18,801,310	3,259,602	17.3
NY	19,378,102	2,617,943	13.5
TX	25,145,561	2,601,886	10.3
PA	12,702,379	1,959,307	15.4

The older population portion of the 2010 United States Census was used to narrow the sample population to five states with the highest number of older adults in those states.[1] According to the 2010 United States Census, the five states are California, Florida, New York, Texas, and Pennsylvania (see table 1A).

The number of older adults, rather than percentage of older adults to state population, was chosen as criteria to allow for greater generalizability of the study. Out of 40.2 million, 14.6 million or 36.4 percent of older adults in America live in these five states. In addition, Texas and Florida attract high numbers of retired grandparents, and it is important to include the perspective of retirees in this study.

In order to most effectively establish a sample population for this study, I randomly generated a list of all churches registered with the Evangelical Free Church of America for each of the five states chosen for this study. Five churches were invited to participate in this study as determined by the first church listed from each state using random generation.

I contacted a pastor from each church by email to request inclusion in the study and asked them to provide a list of grandparents for participation. Beginning at the top of the list, I contacted every third grandparent for the study until I interviewed a total of five grandparents from each state. I interviewed twenty-five grandparents for this study, distributed between the participating churches. Interviews occurred by phone. The interviews consisted of three primary sections, each with four to eight questions. Interviews lasted approximately 60 minutes. In order to participate, grandparents were required to have at least one grandchild under the age of 18 years and greater than the age of 18 months. The questions were designed to identify the grandparents' perception of their role, any variation in role due to life factors, and to gauge any spiritual practices the grandparents were performing on a regular basis. Grandparents were asked a series of questions about their relationship with their grandchildren and about their role in their grandchildren's life. The outcome was a list of four roles of grandparents in evangelical contexts, which allows for comparison of those roles with the responsibilities given to grandparents in the Bible.

Population

The population for the second phase of the study was grandparents who profess evangelical faith, are either single or married (man or woman), have at least one grandchild under the age of 18 years and greater than the age of 18 months, and are part of their extended family through birth or adoption.

Sample and Delimitations

For the second phase, the research population was narrowed through a combination of purposive sampling and random sampling. Five states were selected based on 2010 US Census information and older adult demographics. Further narrowing of the population occurred as random sampling was taken of evangelical churches in the five states with the highest population of older adults. Only churches registered with the Evangelical Free Church of America were considered for this study.

Prior to working with the EFCA, I attempted to conduct research through the NAE. I made multiple requests with the NAE to provide a list of member churches in the five states selected for study. The NAE declined to participate. The office manager stated that they were not able to accommodate the request due to a need to protect the privacy of affiliate churches. I provided additional information about myself, the nature of the study, and SBTS. In addition, I provided personal and professional references along with assurances of privacy. After further consideration, the NAE once again declined to participate.

The EFCA was chosen for this study because they share a similar doctrinal alignment with the NAE. The EFCA website claims, "We are committed to Jesus Christ, to the gospel and to one another." In addition, the EFCA is committed to teaching biblical truth and has a high view of Scripture. The EFCA was formed in 1884 when several evangelical churches joined together based on shared doctrine and values. The EFCA website also claims that one of the shared values from the early years of the EFCA was "caring for the elderly." As a result of both doctrine and value, the EFCA was utilized as a sample population for research related to this dissertation.

The research sample for the second phase was delimited to grandparents as defined in chapter 1 (evangelical, married, man or woman, with biological or adopted grandchildren), who are members of their church. Church membership delimitation helped to identify which grandparents perceive themselves to be evangelical. Membership is not granted to non-Christians or to those who do not agree with the core doctrinal beliefs of the church. It is the assumption of this study that evangelical free churches would only allow evangelical, born-again Christians to be members of their church. Therefore, it was highly likely that all individuals nominated were Christians who profess evangelical belief and provided the desired data for study.

The research sample of the second phase consisted of select grandparents in evangelical contexts who have at least one grandchild who is between the age of 18 months and 18 years old. This delimitation was crucial as it ensured the sample included active grandparents that not in a stage of life when grandparenthood was anticipatory or reflective in nature. The research sample included some grandparents who have grandchildren younger than 18 months old and older than 18 years old, but only after it was determined they had a grandchild that fit into the demographic age for the study.

The research sample of grandparents in evangelical contexts was generated from lists provided by pastors at churches randomly selected for participation in the study. I contacted pastors by email and asked them to provide the names of grandparents who are members of their church and have at least one grandchild between the age of 18 months and 18 years old. I asked pastors to eliminate all other grandparents that did not fit the demographic requirements from consideration. If a pastor declined participation or did not respond after multiple inquiries, then I contacted the next church at the top of the randomly generated list for that state. A total of 20 churches were contacted in five different states. Eight pastors agreed to participate and provided the names of grandparents who profess evangelical faith for the study.

The study was confined to the churches selected through random sampling. The study was also confined to the grandparents identified in each of those churches by their pastor. This phase of the study was further confined to grandparents who are members of their church and who have at least one grandchild under the age of 18 years but greater than 18 months old.

Limitations and Generalizations

Numerous factors impacted the generalizability of this study. Approximately 36 percent of Americans 65 and older live in the five states chosen for this study. The purposefully selected states are geographically scattered throughout the United States in order to ensure that the results are not limited to only one region of the United States. Texas and Florida, both included in this study, attract high numbers of retired grandparents and therefore make them critical to include in the study.[2]

Generalizability will be limited to grandparents within the Evangelical Free Church of America. Grandparents who do not believe in the authority, inerrancy, or sufficiency of the Bible are not likely to find this study applicable to themselves. Portions of the study will be generalizable to grandparents who fit certain demographics such as living proximity to grandchildren or the health of the grandparent. Generalizability will also be limited to churches or denominations that share a similar doctrinal alignment with the Evangelical Free Church. This study will not be generalizable to every family and congregation in every setting, but the findings may be transferable or valuable to families who wish to grandparent according to the Bible.

Research Instrumentation

The instrumentation for the second phase of the study contained two stages. The instrument for the first stage was a validated tool from *The Meaning of Grandparenthood* by Helen Kivnick, which measures "social-demographic items, chosen for relevance to grandparenthood meaning."[3] Scholars such as Arthur Kornhaber have recognized that Kivnick's instrument "contained an excellent design for studying grandparenthood that many researchers use today."[4] Demographic questions included age, marital status, education, work status, work classification, household compensation, age-segregated household, current health, parent age, number of children, grandparent age, and number of grandchildren.[5] I added one additional demographic question: living proximity to grandchildren. This portion of the instrument provided key demographic information and allowed me to determine if certain demographics influence variation in grandparent function.

The instrument for stage 2 was used to interview grandparents from churches selected for this study. I conducted interviews by phone, as geographical location did not permit face-to-face interviews. I recorded interviews, using TapeACall, with the permission of each grandparent. The purpose of the interviews was to determine a list of four to six roles that Christian grandparents operate from, and to compare these roles with a biblical portrait of grandparenthood and sociological literature on grandparent roles. In addition, the interviews identified the spiritual practices that Christian grandparents utilize as they interact with their grandchildren.

I refined the interview questions multiple times with the assistance of Robin Jeffers, who is the Coordinator of Assessment from Bellevue College.[6] I gave Jeffers a proposed list of questions (see appendix 1). The instrument contained three sections, each meant to answer one research question. Each section originally had six or more questions. Jeffers's recommendations included the following: (1) reduce the number of primary questions in each section; (2) add probing questions for added clarity; and (3) reword a number of the questions so they are open-ended. Jeffers encouraged me to pilot test the updated version of the instrument.

I conducted a pilot test on two grandparents who profess evangelical faith. The pilot tests revealed that additional changes were necessary for the instrument. First, research questions needed to focus more specifically around the biblical themes of grandparenthood from the biblical portion of the study. Interview questions needed to be refined to enable me to evaluate a grandparent according to biblical themes identified in the first phase of the study. I found the following themes in the biblical portion of the study, but not in the pilot study: the value of grandchildren, the grandparent's role in the salvation of a grandchild, the grandparent's role in leaving a financial inheritance, and the grandparent's devotional practices. Two additional themes were added to the pilot study that were not found in the biblical portrait but were deemed important for the research: the grandparent's role in the local church and ways the grandparent's church equipped them to disciple grandchildren.

Second, after the conclusion of the pilot study, three questions were removed as they did not specifically answer the primary research questions of the dissertation. These questions include: "The biggest challenge you think your grandchildren face today and why you think that is a challenge." "What do you consider to be the three most important things for you to be doing in your grandchildren's lives?" And, "What do you consider to be the measure of success for a grandparent?"

I refined the instrument by adding the following questions: (1) Describe practices in your life that demonstrate the value you place on grandparenting. (2) How important is it to you that your children have grandchildren? (3) What do you consider to be your role as a grandparent with your children and grandchildren? (4) What do you consider to be your role as a grandparent at your local church? (5) What do you consider to be your role as a grandparent in the salvation of your grandchildren? (6) What do you consider to be your role as a grandparent in the spiritual growth of your grandchildren? (7) What do you consider to be your responsibility as a grandparent in leaving a financial inheritance for your grandchildren? (8) What do you consider to be your role as a grandparent with your grandchildren during retirement years? (9) Tell me about your devotional practices. Describe how you are trying to pass that on to your grandchildren. (10) Could you tell me some ways your church has equipped you to disciple your grandchildren? I conducted a final pilot test utilizing the updated instrument. Results confirmed that no additional changes to the instrument were necessary (see appendix 2 for Jeffers' letter of approval of research protocol).

Research interviews consisted of three open-ended questions that were general in nature, followed by specific probes designed to prompt responses that revealed the interviewees' beliefs, values, and practices. The research instrument addressed three dimensions: (1) the grandparent's relationship with grandchildren; (2) the perceived role as expressed by the grandparent; and (3) the practices grandparents use to engage with grandchildren. Each grandparent was interviewed separately, with a fairly equal distribution of men (13) and women (12). Grandparents were asked a variety of open-ended questions regarding their relationship to their grandchild: how often and on what occasions they see their grandchildren; what the significance and meaning of grandparenthood is in their lives and how it affects them; what the role of a grandparent is in the lives of their grandchildren; and what they are doing to nurture the faith of their children and grandchildren.

Notes

1. The US Census does not measure stage of life (i.e., grandparenthood), but age. This limitation required me to choose age as to the means to determine the sample population.

2. Based on the results of the study, it was clear that the choice of states did not bias the data. A number of states included in the study attract large numbers of grandparents who relocate to warm climates. No grandparent from the population sample relocated for leisure or weather and only one of twenty-five grandparents relocated across the country to live close to their children. The remainder of the grandparents in the sample population lived in the state where they raised their family.

3. Helen Kivnick, *The Meaning of Grandparenthood* (Ann Arbor, MI: UMI Research Press, 1982), 26.

4. Arthur Kornhaber, *Contemporary Grandparenting* (Thousand Oaks, CA: Sage, 1996), 8.

5. Kivnick, *The Meaning of Grandparenthood*, 91-94.

6. Robin Jeffers was awarded The Anna Sue MacNeill Award for Lifetime Achievement in Assessment, Teaching, and Learning. Jeffers's emphasis is the design of qualitative assessment questions, coding text, and organizing by theme so that inferences can be made of the data.

APPENDIX 4

Demographic and Sample Data

The demographic portion of the survey allowed me to determine if certain demographics influence variation in grandparent function. The demographic topics and design were created by Helen Kivnick; her method is recognized as a good design and is utilized by researchers today. Demographic questions include age, marital status, education, work status, household composition, age-segregated household, current health, parenthood age, number of children, grandparenthood age, and number of grandchildren (see tables 2A to 12A). One additional demographic question was added: living proximity to grandchildren (see table 13A).

I interviewed a total of 25 grandparents from five different states. The grandparents differ greatly in age, stage of life, living proximity to grandchildren, and number of grandchildren. Number of grandchildren per grandparent ranged from 2 to 38. The age at which an individual became a grandparent ranged from the mid-30s to the late-50s. The tables below provide a picture of some life factors that may or may not impact a grandparent's ability to invest in a grandchild.

Table 2A. Age

Question	45-54	55-64	65-74	75-84	84+
What is your age range?	2	9	13	0	1

Table 3A. Marital status

Question	Single	Married	Separated	Divorced	Widowed
What is your marital status?	0	25	0	4 (all re-married)	0

Table 4A. Education

Question	0-8	9-11	12-13	2yr C	4yr C	MA	Doc
Level of education?	0	0	2	5	14	3	1

Table 5A. Work status

Question	For pay	Household	Retired
What is your work status?	2	9	13

Table 6A. Household composition

Question	Live Alone	Live with Spouse	Child or Grandchild Lives With You	Other
What is your household composition?	0	25	5	0

Table 7A. Age-segregated household

Question	Yes	No
Do you live with your child or grandchild?	0	25

Table 8A. Current health

Question	Excellent	Good	Fair	Poor
What is the current state of your health?	18	5	2	0

Table 9A. Parenthood age range

Question	Under 20	20-24	25-29	30-34	34+
What age range did you become a parent?	2	9	12	2	0

Table 10A. Number of children

Question	1	2-3	4-5	6+
How many children do you have?	0	16	4	5

Table 11A. Grandparenthood age range

Question	<30	31-40	41-45	45-50	51-55	56-60	61-65	66-70	71+
Age when became a grandparent?	0	1	3	7	10	4	0	0	0

Table 12A. Number of grandchildren

Question	1	2-3	4-6	7-9	10-15	16+
How many grandchildren do you have?	0	6	10	3	5	2

Table 13A. Living proximity to grandchildren

Question	0-20 miles	21-100 miles	101-300 miles	301-500 miles	500+ miles
How many miles do you live from your grandchildren?	17	7	4	4	9

Note. Number exceeds 25 due to grandparents who have multiple grandchildren living in different locations.

Bibliography

"Age Old Intestate." *Harper's Magazine* 162 (May 1931): 712-14.

Ajayi, Joel A. A. *A Biblical Theology of Gerassapience*. New York: Peter Lang, 2010.

Aldous, Joan. "New Views of Grandparents in Intergenerational Context." *Journal of Family Issues* 16, no. 1 (1995): 104-22.

Allen, Holly Catterton. "Bringing the Generations Back Together: Introduction to Intergenerationality." *Christian Education Journal* 9, no. 1 (2012): 101-4.

_____. "God across the Generations: The Spiritual Influence of Grandparents." In *Nurturing Children's Spirituality: Christian Perspectives and Best Practices,* edited by Holly Catterton Allen, 267-83. Eugene, OR: Wipf and Stock, 2008.

Allen, Holly Catterton, with Heidi Schultz Oschwald. "The Spiritual Influence of Grandparents." *Christian Education Journal* 5, no. 2 (2008): 347-62.

Allen, Holly Catterton, and Christine Lawton Ross. *Intergenerational Christian Formation*. Downers Grove, IL: InterVarsity, 2012.

Andrews, Edward M. "Finding Peace in Successful Aging." *New Theological Review* 23, no. 4 (2010): 13-20.

Anthony, Michael, and Michelle Anthony. *A Theology for Family Ministry*. Nashville: B & H, 2011.

Apple, Dorrian. "The Social Structure of Grandparenthood," *American Anthropologist* 58, no. 4 (1956): 656-63.

Baker, Lindsey A., Merril Silverstein, and Norella M. Putney. "Grandparents Raising Grandchildren in the United States: Changing Family Forms, Stagnant Social Policies." *J Soc Policy* 7 (2008): 53-69.

Baldwin, Gary. "Heritage." In *Holman Illustrated Bible Dictionary*. Edited by Charles W. Draper, Chad Brand, and Archie England. Nashville: Holman Bible, 2003.

Barranti, Chrystal C. Ramirez. "The Grandparent/Grandchild Relationship: Family Resource in an Era of Voluntary Bonds." *Family Relations* 34, no. 3 (1985): 343-52.

Bebbington, W. David. *Evangelicalism in Modern Britain: A History from the 1730s to the 1980s*. Florence, KY: Routledge, 1989.

Bengtson, Vern L. "Beyond the Nuclear Family: The Increasing Importance of Multigenerational Bonds." *Journal of Marriage and Family* 63, no. 1 (2001): 1-16.

_____. "Diversity and Symbolism in Grandparents' Role." In *Grandparenthood*, edited by Vern L. Bengtson and Joan F. Robertson, 11-25. Beverly Hills: Sage, 1985.

Bengtson, Vern L., and Joan F. Robertson. *Grandparenthood*. Beverly Hills: Sage, 1985.

Bernal, Jeronimo Gonzalez, and Raquel de la Fuente Anuncibay. "Intergenerational Grandparent/Grandchild Relations: The Socioeducational Role of Grandparents." *Educational Gerontology* 34 (2008): 67-88.

Biddle, Mark E. *Missing the Mark: Sin and Its Consequences in Biblical Theology.* Nashville: Abingdon, 2005.

Bjorklund, David F., and Anthony D. Pellegrini. "Child Development and Evolutionary Psychology." *Child Development* 71, no. 6 (2000): 1687-1708.

Blechman, Andrew D. *Leisureville: Adventures in a World without Children.* New York: Grove, 2008.

Blidstein, Gerald. *Honor Thy Father and Mother.* New York: KTAV Publishing House, 1975.

Bly, Steven, and Janet Bly. *The Power of a Godly Grandparent: Leaving a Spiritual Legacy.* Kansas City, MO: Beacon Hill, 2003.

Bogdan, Robert C., and Sari Knopp Bilkin. *Qualitative Research for Education: An Introduction to Theory and Methods.* Needham Heights, MA: Allyn and Bacon, 1992.

Boice, James Montgomery. *Genesis 1-11: Creation and Fall.* Grand Rapids: Baker, 1992.

_____. *Psalms 1-41.* Grand Rapids: Baker, 1994.

_____. *Psalms 42-106.* Grand Rapids: Baker, 1996.

Boyd, Rosamonde. "The Valued Grandparent: A Changing Social Role." In *Living in the Multigenerational Family,* edited by W. Donohue, J. Kornbluh, and B. Powers, 1-11. Ann Arbor, MI: Institute of Gerontology, 1969.

Bradley, Reb. "Biblical Insights into Child Training." Accessed February 14, 2014. http://www.gracegems.org/2010/03/baby.html.

Brierley, Peter. *Reaching and Keeping Tweenagers.* London: Christian Research, 2002.

Brown, Beth E. "Spiritual Formation in Older Adults." In *The Christian Educator's Handbook on Spiritual Formation,* edited by Kenneth O. Gangel and James C. Wilhoit, 258-68. Grand Rapids: Baker, 1994.

Brown, Francis, S. R. Driver, and Charles A. Briggs. *Enhanced Brown-Driver-Briggs Hebrew and English Lexicon.* Electronic ed. Oak Harbor, WA: Logos Research Systems, 2000.

Brown, Raymond. *The Message of Deuteronomy.* The Bible Speaks Today Commentary Series. Downers Grove, IL: InterVarsity, 1993.

Browning, W. R. F. "Old Age." In *Oxford Dictionary of the Bible.* New York: Oxford University Press, 2009.

Burns, J. Patout. *Theological Anthropology.* Philadelphia: Fortress, 1981.

Calvin, John. *Commentary on the Psalms.* Edited by David C. Searle. Carlisle: Banner of Truth Trust, 2009.

_____. *Genesis.* The Crossway Classic Commentaries. Wheaton, IL: Crossway, 2001.

Caragounis, Chrys S. "b n." In *New International Dictionary of Theology and Exegesis.* Edited by Willem A. VanGemeren. Grand Rapids: Zondervan, 1997.

Charles, Don C. "Literary Old Age: A Browse through History." *Educational Gerontology* 2, no. 3 (1977): 237-53.

Cherlin, Andrew J., and Frank F. Furstenberg. *The New American Grandparent: A Place in the Family, a Life Apart.* Cambridge, MA: Harvard University Press, 1992.

_____. "Styles and Strategies of Grandparenting." In *Grandparenthood,* edited by Vern L. Bengtson and Joan F. Robertson, 97-116. Beverly Hills, CA: Sage, 1985.

Clavan, Sylvia. "The Impact of Social Class and Social Trends on the Role of the Grandparent." *Family Coordinator* 27, no. 4 (1978): 351-57.

Clements, Ronald. *Exodus,* The Cambridge Bible Commentary. London: Cambridge University Press, 1972.

Cloyd, Betty Shannon. *Parents & Grandparents as Spiritual Guides.* Nashville: Upper Room, 2000.

Coall, David A., and Ralph Hertwig. "Grandparental Investment: Past, Present, Future." *Behavioral and Brain Sciences* 33 (2010): 1-59.

Cochran, M. M., and J. A. Brassard. "Child Development and Personal Social Networks." *Child Development* 50 (1979): 601-16.

Conrad, J. "z gén." In *Theological Dictionary of the Old Testament.* Edited by G. Johannes Botterweck and Helmer Ringgren. Grand Rapids: Eerdmans, 1980.

Conroy, Donald B., and Charles J. Fahey. "Christian Perspectives on the Role of Grandparents." In *Grandparenthood,* edited by Vern L. Bengtson and Joan F. Robertson, 195-207. Beverly Hills: Sage, 1985.

Copen, Casey, and Merril Silverstein. "Transmission of Religious Beliefs across the Generations: Do Grandparents Matter?" *Journal of Comparative Family Studies* 38, no. 4 (2007): 497-510.

Creswell, John W. *Qualitative Inquiry & Research Design: Choosing among Five Approaches.* Thousand Oaks, CA: Sage, 1992.

Davies, James. "A Practical Theology of Aging: Biblical Perspectives for Individuals and the Church." *Christian Education Journal* 5, no. 2 (2008): 275-93.

Day, John. "Pre-Deuteronomic Allusions to the Covenant in Hosea and Psalm 78." *Vetus Testamentum* 36, no. 1 (1986): 1-12.

Dempster, Stephen G. *Dominion and Dynasty: A Theology of the Hebrew Bible.* Edited by D. A. Carson. Downers Grove, IL: InterVarsity, 2003.

Denham, Thomas E., and Craig W. Smith. "The Influence of Grandparents on Grandchildren: A Review of the Literature and Resources." *Family Relations* 38, no. 3 (1989): 345-50.

Dockery, David S., and Gregory Alan Thornbury. *Shaping a Christian Worldview: The Foundation of Christian Higher Education.* Nashville: B & H, 2002.

Drane, J. W. "Family." In *New Dictionary of Biblical Theology: Exploring the Unity & Diversity of Scripture.* Edited by. T. Desmond Alexander, Brian S. Rosner, D. A. Carson, and Graeme Goldsworthy. Downers Grove, IL: InterVarsity, 2000.

Dunifon, Rachel, and Ashish Bajracharya. "The Role of Grandparents in the Lives of Youth." *Journal of Family Issues* 33, no. 9 (2012): 1168-94.

Durham, John. *Exodus.* Word Biblical Commentary, vol. 3. Nashville: Thomas Nelson, 1987.

Eichler, J. "Inheritance." In *New International Dictionary of New Testament Theology.* Edited by Colin Brown. Grand Rapids: Zondervan, 1976.

Ellingson, Dennis, and Kit Ellingson. *The Godly Grandparent: Living Faithfully and Influencing your Grandchildren for Christ.* Greeley, CO: CLADACH, 2007.

Enns, Peter. *Exodus.* The NIV Application Commentary. Grand Rapids: Zondervan, 2000.

Estes, Daniel. "Like Arrows in the Hands of a Warrior." *Vetus Testamentum* 41, no. 3 (1991): 304-11.

Evangelical Free Church of America. "Who We Are." Accessed October 5, 2012. www.efca.org/explore/who-we-are.

Fisher, Bradley J. "Successful Aging, Life Satisfaction, and Generativity in Later Life." *International Journal of Aging and Human Development* 41, no. 3 (1995): 239-50.

Foerster, Werner. "Inheritance." In *Theological Dictionary of the New Testament*. Edited by Gerhard Kittel and Gerhard Friedrich. Grand Rapids: William B. Eerdmans, 1964.

Fox, Michael V. "Aging and Death in Qohelet 12." *Journal for the Study of the Old Testament* 42 (1988): 55-77.

Friedman, Debra, and Michael Hechter. "Motivating Grandparent Investment." *Behavioral and Brain Sciences* 33, no. 1 (2010): 24-25.

Gardner, Christine J. "Finishing Well: After Achieving Success, Early Retirees Are Finding Significance in Second-Career Mission Assignments." *Christianity Today* 42, no. 11 (1998): 72-75.

Garland, Diana R. *Family Ministry: A Comprehensive Guide.* Downers Grove, IL: IVP, 1999.

Goodrick, Edward W., and John R. Kohlenberger. *Zondervan NIV Exhaustive Concordance.* 2nd ed. Grand Rapids: Zondervan, 1999.

Gratton, Brian, and Carole Haber. "Three Phases in the History of American Grandparents: Authority, Burden, Companion." *Generations* 20, no. 1 (1996): 7-13.

Gudorf, Christine E. "How to Be Great Grandparents: The Joys and Challenges of Grandparents Today." *U.S. Catholic* 67 (July 2002): 18-19.

Hagestad, Gunhild O. "Continuity and Connectedness." In *Grandparenthood,* edited by Vern L. Bengtson and Joan F. Robertson, 31-48. Beverly Hills, CA: Sage, 1985.

————. "Problems and Promises in the Social Psychology of Intergenerational Relations." In *Aging: Stability and Change in the Family,* edited by R. Fogel, E. Hatfield, S. Kiesler, and R. Shanas, 11-46. New York: Academic Press, 1981.

Harper, Cavin. *Courageous Grandparenting: Unshakable Faith in a Broken World.* Colorado Springs: Christian Grandparenting Network, 2013.

Harper, Sarah. "The Challenge for Families of Demographic Ageing." In *Families in Ageing Societies,* edited by Sarah Harper, 6-30. Oxford: Oxford University Press, 2004.

Harper, Sarah, and Iva Ruicheva. "Grandmothers as Replacement Parents and Partners: The Role of Grandmotherhood in Single Parent Families." *Journal of Intergenerational Relationships* 8, no. 3 (2010): 219-33.

Harrington, Michael. *The Older America: Poverty in the United States.* Baltimore: Penguin Books, 1962.

Harris, J. Gordon. *Biblical Perspectives on Aging: God and the Elderly.* New York: Haworth, 2008.

Harris, R. Laird. *Leviticus.* In vol. 2 of *The Expositor's Bible Commentary.* Edited by Frank E. Gaebelein, 499-654. Grand Rapids: Zondervan, 1990.

Hay, David, and Rebecca Nye. *The Spirit of the Child.* Rev. ed. Philadelphia: Jessica Kingsley, 2006.

Hayslip, Bert, and Julie H. Patrick. *Custodial Grandparenting: Individual, Cultural and Ethnic Diversity.* New York: Springer, 2006.

Henry, Matthew. *A Church in the House*. San Antonio: The Vision Forum, 2007.

Hess, Beth B. "America's Age Revisited: Who, What, When, and Why?" In *Growing Old in America*, edited by Beth B. Hess, 1-18. New Brunswick, NJ: Rutgers University Press, 1980.

Hester, James D. *Paul's Concept of Inheritance: A Contribution to the Understanding of Heilsgeschichte*. Edinburgh: Oliver and Boyd, 1968.

Heywood, Elizabeth M. "Custodial Grandparents and Their Grandchildren." *Family Journal* 7, no. 4 (1999): 367-71.

Hostetter, Edwin C. "Fruitful." In *New International Dictionary of Theology and Exegesis*. Edited by Willem A. VanGemeren. Grand Rapids: Zondervan, 1997.

Houston, James M., and Michael Parker. *A Vision for the Aging Church: Renewing Ministry for and by Seniors*. Downers Grove, IL: IVP, 2011.

Howell, Trevor H. "King Solomon's Portrait of Old Age." *Age and Aging* 16, no. 5 (1987): 331-33.

Isenberg, Sheldon. "Aging in Judaism: 'Crown of Glory' and 'Days of Sorrow.'" In *Handbook of the Humanities and Aging*, edited by Thomas R. Cole, David D. van Tassel, and Robert Kastenbaum, 149-74. New York: Springer, 1992.

Johnson, Colleen L. "Grandparenting Options in Divorcing Families: An Anthropological Perspective." In *Grandparenthood*, edited by Vern L. Bengtson and Joan F. Robertson, 81-96. Beverly Hills: Sage, 1985.

Jones, Timothy Paul. "Intergenerational Faithfulness." *The Journal of Discipleship & Family Ministry* 3, no. 2 (2013): 8-35.

Kahana, Boaz, and Eva Kahana. "Grandparenthood from the Perspectives of the Developing Grandchild." *Developmental Psychology* 3, no. 1 (1970): 98-105.

_____. "Theoretical and Research Perspectives on Grandparenthood." *Aging and Human Development* 2, no. 4 (1971): 261-68.

Kemp, Candace L. "The Social Demographic Contours of Contemporary Grandparenthood: Mapping Patterns in Canada and the United States." *Journal of Comparative Studies* 34, no. 2 (2003): 187-213.

King, Sharon V., Elisabeth O. Burgess, Makunga Akinyela, Margret Counts Spriggs, and NeSonya Parker. "The Religious Dimension of the Grandparent Role in Three-Generation African American Households." *Journal of Religion, Spirituality & Aging* 19, no. 1 (2006): 75-96.

Kittler, Keith. "Who Says Grandparents Matter?" *Journal of Beliefs and Values* 29, no. 1 (2008): 51-60.

Kivnic, Helen. "Grandparenthood: An Overview of Meaning and Mental Health." *Gerontologist* 22, no. 1 (1982): 59-66.

_____. "Grandparenthood and Mental Health: Meaning, Behavior, and Satisfaction." In *Grandparenthood*, edited by Vern L. Bengtson and Joan F. Robertson, 151-58. Beverly Hills: Sage, 1985.

_____. *The Meaning of Grandparenthood*. Ann Arbor, MI: UMI Research Press, 1982.

Knierim, Rolf. "Age and Aging in the Old Testament." In *Ministry with the Aging: Designs, Challenges, Foundations*, edited by William Clements, 29. New York: Harper & Row, 1981.

Knight, Douglas A., "Perspectives on Aging and the Elderly in the Hebrew Bible." *Interpretation: A Journal of Bible and Theology* 68, no. 2 (2014): 136-149.

Koehler, Ludwig, and Walter Baumgartner, eds. *The Hebrew and Aramaic Lexicon of the Old Testament.* Vol. 1. Boston: Brill, 2001.

Kornhaber, Arthur. *Contemporary Grandparenting.* Thousand Oaks, CA: Sage, 1996.

_____. *The Grandparent Solution: How Parents Can Build a Family Team for Practical, Emotional, and Financial Success.* San Francisco: Jossey-Boss, 2004.

Kornhaber, Arthur, and Kenneth L. Woodward. *Grandparents/Grandchildren: The Vital Connection.* Garden City, NY: Anchor /Doubleday, 1981.

Köstenberger Andreas J., and David W. Jones. *God, Marriage, and Family: Rebuilding the Biblical Foundation.* Wheaton, IL: Crossway, 2010.

Kraus, Hans~Joachim. *Psalms 60-150.* A Continental Commentary. Minneapolis: Fortress, 1993.

Longman, Tremper III. *Proverbs.* Baker Commentary on the Old Testament Wisdom and Psalms. Grand Rapids: Baker, 2006.

Louw, Johannes P., and Eugene Albert Nida. *Greek-English Lexicon of the New Testament: Based on Semantic Domains.* Electronic ed. New York: Logos Research Systems, 1996.

Luscher, Kurt, and Karl Pillemer. "Intergenerational Ambivalence: A New Approach to the Study of Parent-Child Relationships in Later Life." *Journal of Marriage and the Family* 60, no. 2 (1998): 1-32.

MacArthur, John F. *The Fulfilled Family.* Chicago: Moody Press, 1981.

Madvig, Donald H. *Joshua.* In vol. 3 of *The Expositor's Bible Commentary.* Edited by Frank E. Gaebelein, 237-371. Grand Rapids: Zondervan, 1992.

Marshall, I. Howard. *The Pastoral Epistles.* The International Critical Commentary. New York: T & T Clark, 1999.

Martin-Achard, Robert. "Biblical Perspectives on Aging." In *Aging, Concilium 1991/3,* edited by Lisa Sowle Cahill and Dietmar Mieth, 31-38. Philadelphia: Trinity, 1991.

McIntosh, Gary. "Trends and Challenges for Ministry among North America's Largest Generation." *Christian Education Journal* 5, no. 2 (2008): 294-304.

McKenzie, John L. "The Elders of the Old Testament." *Biblica* 40 (1959): 522.

Meeks, James A. "The Riches of His Inheritance." *Presbyterian* 28, no. 1 (2008): 34-46.

Mills, Doreen Maria. "A Pastoral Theological Response to Grandparents Parenting Grandchildren." Th.M. thesis, Southern Baptist Theological Seminary, 1998.

Minois, Georges. *History of Old Age.* Chicago: University of Chicago Press, 1989.

Mohler, Albert. "The Sins of the Father." December 14, 2010. Accessed June 25, 2014. http://www.albertmohler.com/2010/12/14/the-sins-of-the-father/.

Morrow, Francis J., Jr. "Psalm 21:10: An Example of Haplography." *Vetus Testamentum* 18, no. 4 (1968): 558-59.

Morse, Jennifer Roback. *Love & Economics: It Takes a Family to Raise a Village.* San Marcos, CA: Ruth Institute, 2009.

Mueller, Margaret M., and Glen H. Elder. "Family Contingencies across the Generations: Grandparent-Grandchild Relationship in Holistic Perspective." *Journal of Marriage and Family* 65, no. 2 (2003): 404-17.

Muller, Carl. *Unconverted Sons and Daughters: Hope for Hurting Parents*. Leominster, UK: Day One, 2012.

Mulvihill, Josh. "A New Way of Life for the Old," *Journal of Discipleship and Family Ministry* 3, no. 2 (spring 2013): 24-35.

Murphy, Roland E. *Proverbs*. Word Biblical Commentary, vol. 22. Nashville: Thomas Nelson, 1998.

Nadel, Siegfried Frederick. *The Social Foundations of Social Anthropology*. Glencoe, NY: Free Press, 1951.

National Association of Evangelicals. "What Is an Evangelical." Accessed October 5, 2012. hwww.nae.net/church-and-faith-partners/what-is-an-evangelical.

Neugarten, Bernice L., and Karol K. Weinstein. "The Changing American Grandparent." *Journal of Marriage and Family* 26, no. 2 (1964): 199-204.

Nguyen, vanThanh. "Biblical Perspectives on Caring for the Aged and the Sick." *New Theology Review* 23, no. 4 (2010): 5-12.

Pettigrew, Hal. "Perspectives on the Spiritual Development of the 'Aging' Boomers." *Christian Education Journal* 5, no. 2 (2008): 305-20.

Piper, John. *Rethinking Retirement: Finishing Life for the Glory of Christ*. Wheaton, IL: Crossway, 2009.

Piper, Noel. *Treasuring God in Our Traditions*. Wheaton, IL: Crossway, 2007.

Reitzes, Donald C., and Elizabeth J. Mutran. "Grandparent Identity, Intergenerational Family Identity, and Well-Being." *The Journals of Gerontology: Psychological and Social Sciences* 59B, no. 4 (2004a): 213-19.

————. "Grandparenthood: Factors Influencing Frequency of Grandparent-Grandchildren Contact and Grandparent Role Satisfaction." *The Journals of Gerontology: Psychological and Social Sciences* 59B, no. 1 (2004b): 9-16.

"The Retirement City: A New Way of Life for the Old." *Time Magazine*, August 1962. Accessed October 5, 2012. www.time.com/time/magazine/article/0,9171, 896472,00.html.

Reynolds, Glenda Phillips, James V. Wright, and Betty Beale. "The Roles of Grandparents in Educating Today's Children." *Journal of Instructional Psychology* 30 (2003): 316-25.

Rienow, Rob. *Visionary Parenting: Capture a God-Sized Vision for Your Family*. Nashville: Randall House, 2009.

Roberto, John. "Our Future Is Intergenerational." *Christian Education Journal* 9, no. 1 (2012): 105-20.

Robertson, Joan F. "Grandmotherhood: A Study of Role Conceptions." *The Journal of Marriage and the Family* 39, no. 1 (1977): 165-74.

————. "Interaction in Three Generation Families, Parents as Mediators: Toward a Theoretical Perspective." *International Journal of Aging and Human Development* 6, no. 2 (1975): 103-10.

————. "Significance of Grandparents: Perceptions of Young Adult Grandchildren." *Gerontologist* 16, no. 2 (1976): 137-40.

Robertson, Joan F., and V. Wood. "The Significance of Grandparenthood." In *Time, Roles, and Self in Old Age*, edited by Jaber F. Gubrium, 278-302. New York: Human Sciences, 1976.

Ruggles, Steven. "The Decline of Intergenerational Coresidence in the United States. 1850-2000." *Am Social Rev.* 72, no. 6 (2007): 964-89.

Sailhamer, John H. *Genesis.* In vol. 2 of *The Expositor's Bible Commentary.* Edited by Frank E. Gaebelein, 1-284. Grand Rapids: Zondervan, 1990.

Sapp, Steven. *Full of Years: Aging and the Elderly in the Bible and Today.* Nashville: Abingdon, 1987.

Scofield, Michael D., and Peter W. Kalivas. "Forgiving the Sins of the Fathers." *Nature Neuroscience* 16, no. 1 (2013): 4-5.

Seponski, Desiree, and Denise Lewis. "Caring for and Learning from Each Other: A Grounded Theory Study of Grandmothers and Adult Granddaughters." *Journal of Intergenerational Relationships* 7, no. 4 (2009): 390-410.

Shammas, Carol, Marylynn Salmon, and Michel Dahlin. *Inheritance in America: From Colonial Times to the Present.* New Brunswick, NJ: Rutgers University Press, 1987.

Shenton, Andrew K. "Strategies for Ensuring Truthfulness in Qualitative Research Projects." *Education for Information* 22 (2004): 63-75.

Silverman, Philip, and Robert J. Maxwell. "Cross-Cultural Variation in the Status of Old People." In *Old Age in Preindustrial Society*, edited by Peter N. Stearns, 46-69. New York: Holmes & Meier, 1982.

Silverstein, Merril, and Anne Marenco. "How Americans Enact the Grandparent Role Across the Family Life Course." *Journal of Family Issues* 22, no. 4 (2001): 493-522.

Somary, Karen, and George Stricker. "Becoming a Grandparent: A Longitudinal Study of Expectations and Early Experiences as a Function of Sex and Lineage." *The Gerontologist* 38, no. 1 (1998): 53-61.

Stagg, Frank. *The Bible Speaks on Aging.* Nashville: Broadman, 1981.

Steenberg, Wesley Ryan. "Effective Practices for Training Parents in Family Discipleship: A Mixed Methods Study." Ph.D. diss., Southern Baptist Theological Seminary, 2011.

Stelle, Charlie, Christine Fruhauf, Nancy Orel, and Laura Meyer-Landry. "Grandparenting in the 21st Century: Issues in Diversity in Grandparent-Grandchild Relationships." *Journal of Gerontological Social Work* 53, no. 8 (2010): 682-701.

Strauss, Clifford A. "Grandma Made Johnny Delinquent." *American Journal of Orthopsychiatry* 13, no. 2 (1943): 343-46.

Strom, Robert, and Shirley Strom. "Building a Theory of Grandparent Development." *International Journal of Aging and Human Development* 45, no. 4 (1997): 255-86.

Strong, James. "Greek Dictionary of the New Testament." In *Strong's Exhaustive Concordance of the Bible.* Peabody, MA: Hendrickson, 1988.

Stuart, Douglas K. *Exodus.* The New American Commentary, vol. 2. Nashville: B & H, 2006.

Szinovacz, Maximiliane E. "Grandparents Today: A Demographic Profile" *The Gerontologist* 38, no. 1 (1998): 37-52.

_____. "Research on Grandparenting: Needed Refinements in Concepts, Theories, and Methods." In *Handbook on Grandparenting*, edited by Maximiliane E. Szinovacz, 1-22. Westport, CT: Greenwood, 1998.

Thiele, Diane M., and Thomas A. Whelan. "The Nature and Dimension of the Grandparent Role." *Marriage and Family Review* 40, no. 1 (2006): 93-108.

Thomas, Jeanne L. "The Grandparent Role: A Double Bind." *International Journal of Aging and Human Development* 31, no. 3 (1990): 169-77.

Thomas, Robert L. *New American Standard Hebrew-Aramaic and Greek Dictionaries.* Updated ed. Anaheim: Foundation, 1998.

Thomas, William H. *What Are Old People For? How Elders Will Save the World.* Acton, MA: VanderWyk & Burnham, 2004.

Towns, Ruth, and Elmer Towns. *Grandparents of the Bible: What They Can Teach Us about Influencing Children.* 2003. Accessed February 11, 2014. http://elmertowns. com/wp-content/uploads/2014/01/GrandparentsoftheBible.pdf.

Tinsley, Barbara R., and Ross D. Parke. "Grandparents as Support and Socialization Agents." In *Beyond the Dyad*, edited by M. Lewis, 161-94. New York: Plenum, 1984.

Troll, Lillian E. "Grandparents: The Family Watchdogs." In *Family Relationships in Later Life*, edited by T. M. Brubaker, 63-74. Beverly Hills: Sage, 1983.

Tsevat, Matitiahu. "The Death of the Sons of Eli." *Journal of Bible and Religion* 32, no. 4 (1964): 355-58.

U.S. Census Bureau. "The Older Population: 2010." Accessed October 25, 2012. http://www.census.gov/prod/cen2010/briefs/c2010br-09.pdf.

Uhlenberg, Peter, and Bradley Hammill. "Frequency of Grandparent Contact with Grandchildren Sets: Six Factors That Make a Difference." *The Gerontologist* 38, no. 3 (1997): 276-85.

Valentino, Timothy R. "Fight to the Finish: 2 Timothy 4:1-8." *Evangelical Journal* 29, no. 1 (2011): 24-32.

Vanderwell, Howard. *The Church of All Ages.* Herndon, NC: The Alban Institute, 2008.

VanGemeren, Willem A. *Psalms.* In vol. 5 of *The Expositor's Bible Commentary.* Edited by Frank E. Gaebelein, 1-880. Grand Rapids: Zondervan, 1991.

Vollmer, Hermann. "The Grandmother: A Problem in Childrearing." *American Journal of Orthopsychiatry* 7, no. 3 (1937): 378-82.

Waldrop, Deborah P., Joseph Weber, Shondel L. Herald, Julie Pruett, Kathy Cooper, and Kevin Juozapavicius. "Wisdom and Life Experience: How Grandfathers Mentor Their Grandchildren." *Journal of Aging and Identity* 4, no. 1 (1999): 33-46.

Waltke, Bruce K. *The Book of Proverbs: Chapters 1-15.* New International Commentary on the Old Testament. Grand Rapids: William B. Eerdmans, 2004.

Wechsler, Harlan J. "Judiac Perspectives on Grandparenthood." In *Grandparenthood*, edited by Vern L. Bengtson and Joan F. Robertson, 185-94. Beverly Hills: Sage, 1985.

Wegner, Paul D. "Old Age." *New International Dictionary of Theology and Exegesis.* Edited by Willem A. VanGemeren. Grand Rapids: Zondervan, 1997.

Wells, David F. *The Courage to Be Protestant: Truth-Lovers, Marketers, and Emergents in the Postmodern World.* Grand Rapids: William Eerdmans, 2008.

Wenham, Gordon. *Genesis 1-15.* Word Biblical Commentary, vol. 1. Nashville: Thomas Nelson, 1987.

Westermann, Claus. *Genesis 1-11*. A Continental Commentary. Minneapolis: Fortress, 1994.

————. *Genesis 12-36*. A Continental Commentary. Minneapolis: Fortress, 1995.

White, James. *Intergenerational Religious Education: Models, Theory, and Prescription for Interage Life and Learning in the Faith Community*. Birmingham, AL: Religious Education Press, 1988.

Wilhoit, James C. *Spiritual Formation as if the Church Mattered*. Grand Rapids: Baker, 2008.

Williams, Donald. *Mere Humanity*. Nashville: B & H, 2006.

Willis, Timothy M. "Elders in Pre-Exilic Israelite Society." Ph.D. diss., Harvard University, 1990.

Wilson, Alistair I., and Jamie A. Grant. *The God of Covenant: Biblical, Theological, and Contemporary Perspectives*. Downers Grove, IL: InterVarsity, 2005.

Wilson, Keren B., and Michael R. DeShane. "The Legal Rights of Grandparents: A Preliminary Discussion." *The Gerontologist* 22, no. 1 (1982): 67-71.

Wood, A. Skevington. *Ephesians*. In vol. 11 of *The Expositors Bible Commentary*. Edited by Frank Gaebelien, 1-92. Grand Rapids: Zondervan, 1995.

Wood, Vivian. "Grandparenthood: An Ambiguous Role." *Generations: Journal of the Western Gerontological Society* 22 (1982): 18-24.

Wright, Christopher J. H. "The Fathers." In *New International Dictionary of Theology and Exegesis*. Edited by Willem A. VanGemeren. Grand Rapids: Zondervan, 1997.

Wright, J. Stafford. *Ecclesiastes*. In vol. 5 of *The Expositor's Bible Commentary*. Edited by Frank Gaebelein, 1135-97. Grand Rapids: Zondervan, 1991.

Zuck, Roy B. *Precious in His Sight: Childhood & Children in the Bible*. Grand Rapids: Baker, 199

One grandparent can make a difference.

_____

30 million grandparents can influence

GENERATIONS.

The Legacy Coalition is a non-denominational organization committed to helping grandparents love and influence their grandchildren for Christ, and to helping churches minister effectively to the more than 30 million Christian grandparents who need encouragement, training and resources.

LEGACYCOALITION.COM

A MINISTRY OF AWANA